SPECIFIC CHARACTERISTICS OF MENTAL AND SPEECH DEVELOPMENT IN CHILDREN WITH FEBRILE SEIZURES

Gaffarova Visola Furkatovna

© Taemeer Publications LLC
Specific characteristics of Mental and Speech Development in Children with febrile seizures
by: Gaffarova Visola Furkatovna
Edition: August '2023
Publisher:
Taemeer Publications LLC (Michigan, USA / Hyderabad, India)

ISBN 978-93-5872-127-0

© Taemeer Publications

Book	:	Specific characteristics of Mental and Speech Development in Children with febrile seizures
Author	:	Gaffarova Visola Furkatovna
Publisher	:	Taemeer Publications
Year	:	'2023
Pages	:	178
Title Design	:	*Taemeer Web Design*

Bukhara - 2023.

UDK: 616.8-005-616.831.31-008.6

The monograph presents the peculiarities of mental and speech development in children with febrile seizures, a new approach to their diagnosis and complex treatment, a treatment and prevention algorithm to prevent their transition from febrile type to afebrile type. the issues of evaluating the analysis of neuropsychological test indicators, improving the diagnosis and treatment algorithm for preventing the transition of febrile seizures to afebrile type and mental and speech changes in them were studied.

The monograph is intended for scientific researchers, masters, clinical residents and all medical workers.

Author: Gaffarova V.F. - Assistant of the Department of Neurology of the Bukhara State Medical Institute named aFSer Abu Ali Ibn Sina, Ph.D.

Reviewers:

Usmanova D.D. - assistant professor of the Department of Nervous Diseases, Children's Neurological Diseases and Medical Genetics, Tashkent Pediatric Medical Institute, Ph.D.

Urinov M.B. - Associate Professor of the Neurology Department of the Bukhara State Medical Institute named aFSer Abu Ali Ibn Sina, DSc.

Contents:

1.	Introduction	8
	Chapter 1. Contemporary views on febrile seizures in children.	11
	1.1. Issues of epidemiology, etiology and pathogenesis of febrile seizures in children.	
	1.2. Genetic aspects of febrile seizures in children.	
	1.3. Clinical signs and course of febrile seizures in children and ways to optimize their treatment	
	1.4. Diagnosis, differential diagnosis of febrile seizures in children	
	1.5. Diagnostic criteria for transition of febrile seizures to afebrile.	
	1.6. Болаларда фебрил тутқаноқларни даволашга ёндашувлар.	
2.	Chapter 2. - Modern approaches to early diagnosis and treatment of febrile seizures in children. 2.1. General description of children with febrile seizures by gender and age.	36
	2.2 Electroencephalography.	
	2.3. Magnetic resonance imaging	
	2.4. Complex neuropsychological research methods	

3.	Chapter 3. Risk factors for the development of febrile and afebrile seizures in children. clinical course, diagnosis and comparative diagnosis of febrile and afebrile seizures.	51
	3.1. Etiological, clinical-neurological and neurophysiological characteristics of febrile and afebrile seizures	
	Chapter 3 Discussion	
4.	Chapter 4. Results of febrile seizures and their clinical-neurological and neurophysiological description. risk factors predicting the transformation of febrile seizures into afebrile seizures.	78
	4.1. Etiological, clinical-neurological and neurophysiological characteristics of the outcome of febrile seizures.	
	4.2. Risk factors influencing the transition of febrile seizures to epilepsy.	
	4.3. Prognosis of the development of epilepsy	
	Chapter 4 Discussion	
5.	Chapter 5. Data from a comparative comprehensive neuropsychological examination of patients with a history of febrile and afebrile seizures and febrile seizures.	104
	5.1. Data from a comprehensive neuropsychological examination of patients with a positive qualitative	

	outcome of febrile seizures.	
	5.2. Data from a comprehensive neuropsychological examination of patients with febrile seizures ending in epilepsy.	
	Discussion	
6.	Conclusions	138
7.	Reference list	140
8.	List of published scientific works	172
9.	Abbreviations	176

INTRODUCTION

Febrile seizures (seizures, FS) are the most common variant of paroxysmal conditions in pediatric practice today. These episodes of epileptic seizures occur in preschool children with hyperthermia and are not associated with neuroinfection. FS is a benign, age-related, genetically determined condition in which the brain becomes susceptible to epileptic seizures in response to high temperatures. In children of preschool age, FS is considered transient in most cases, but at the same time it can be part of separate epileptic syndromes [Pavlidou E, Panteliadis C.2013., Chung S.2014, Dolinina A.F., Gromova L.L., Mukhin K. Yu., 2015]. The prevalence of febrile seizures in children aged 6 months to 6 years is 2-5% [Ismailova N.B. 2013., Musabekova T.O., 2014, Olimov A.R., 7017.,]. Boys are more affected than girls, with a ratio of 1.5-2:1. The peak of the disease is observed at the age of 18 months. Epilepsy episodes of various etiologies are identified in the family anamnesis of 80% of patients [Dolinina A.F., 2015., Turovskaya 2016]. 25% of children's parents also suffer from similar symptoms in childhood. In most cases, the outcome of the disease is positive and depends on the correct tactics of the doctor. Febrile seizures in children are a heterogeneous pathological condition, in which 17-30% of cases develop epilepsy. The exact etiology and pathogenesis are not defined [Uria-Avettanal C. 2013., Zavadenko A.N. 2016]. One of the possible factors for the development of this pathology is the immaturity of MAT in children under 6 years of age, which is manifested by a tendency to generalize processes and weakness of brake activity [Turovskaya N.G. 2013., Zavadenko A.N. 2016., Kleshchenko 2019]. Diseases occurring in children [Kitaev V.E., Kotov A.S.].

h.Sh. Shamansurov with co-authors, studying the amount of Ca2+ in blood serum, the results of studying the dynamics of changes in febrile and afebrile seizures in early children showed a significant decrease compared to the norm, which is observed with especially gross and expressive neurological disorders, repeated and severe paroxysms, concluded that it is highly expressed in children with afebrile seizures. Currently, most children who have experienced FS are in good health, and the post-seizure condition has a positive quality of life in the setting of a single episode. It should be noted that recently there is evidence that a small proportion of children may develop neurological deficits aFSer FS, relapse of FS or epilepsy, learning problems, movement disorders and behavioral changes, unspecialized sensory symptoms, and memory failure [Manreza M.L., Gherpelli J.L., Machado-Haertel L.R., et al., Berg A.T., Shinnar S. 2010., Wasserman L.I. 2015., Zavadenko A.N. 2016], which requires prompt assistance to children with FS, timely correction of disorders [Sharipov A.M., Olimov A.R., Khakimov J.P. 2017].

The above-mentioned problems are also relevant in the Republic of Uzbekistan, scientific works devoted to this problem are rare in the literature.

Based on the mentioned reasons, it is urgent and necessary to solve the above problems by means of the planned research work.

CHAPTER 1.
MODERN VIEWS OF FEBRILE SEIZURES IN CHILDREN.

1.1. Issues of epidemiology, etiology and pathogenesis of febrile seizures in children.

Seizure syndrome is one of the most urgent problems of children's neurology. The frequency of epilepsy in the population is 0.5-0.75% of the pediatric population, and febrile seizures (FS) - up to 5% [29,101]. Half of all seizures occur before the age of 15, with the most seizures occurring between the ages of 1 and 9. The frequent development of seizures in childhood is explained both by the peculiarities of the child's nervous system and by various reasons that cause them [74]. The conclusion of FS, their risk of progression to an afebrile form, raises further questions [7,153].

A febrile seizure (eng. - febrile seizures) is a tonic or tonic in the limbs in infants, early and preschool children, with a body temperature of not less than 37.8-38.5 oC (except for seizures caused by MAT infection). paroxysms that occur in the form of clonic seizures, of varying duration, and eventually afebrile seizures (ATT) and epilepsy [72,79,89,93]. Preexisting afebrile seizures in the anamnesis of children does not allow seizure episodes occurring on the background of hyperthermia to be accepted as febrile seizures [23,69]. It should be mentioned that FS is a common variant of proximal cases in pediatric practice [2,5,15]. These are episodes of epileptic seizures occurring in preschool children with hyperthermia not associated with neuroinfection [10,15]. K. Yu. According to the definition of Mukhin [13]: "...febrile seizures are a positive qualitative, age-related, genetically determined condition in which the brain is prone to epileptic seizures occurring in response to high temperature. Febrile seizures are usually transient in children of preschool age, but can also be part of separate epileptic syndromes" [6,9,23]. FS is the most common paroxysmal condition among children aged 6 months to 5 years, and belongs to the group of diseases that do not require the diagnosis of epilepsy [42]. The term febrile seizure itself was replaced by febrile seizures in 2001, because in the clinical course of this condition, not only seizures, but also paroxysms without seizures can be observed [52]. ILAE (1993) defines FS as "seizures in children older than 6 months, associated with febrile illness, not caused by MAT infection; does not have previous seizures and unprovoked seizures in the neonatal period, and does not meet the criteria for other acute symptomatic seizures" [47,48].

Information on the prevalence of FS in the literature is abundant and varied. As early as the beginning of the 20th century, FS was reported in 4.2% of children, with 2–4% of children between 6 months and 5 years of age having at least one episode of FS [69,70,71,109].

In recent years, the average incidence of FS in children under 5 years of age is 2-5% [13,24,73,117,134,166], with a slightly higher incidence in boys (estimated ratio 1.4:1) [63,71,81]. Currently, the prevalence of FS in the USA and European countries is around 2–4% [118,152].

The wide range of prevalence is explained by the variety of methods used to define cases and differences in the definition of FS used by researchers [128,160]. It should be noted that it is difficult to statistically consider FS in children, because in the practice of neurology there is no single approach to the diagnosis and consideration of children with this pathology, which, in turn, complicates obtaining reliable data on the prevalence of the disease, as well as another factor is the fact that FS is different from other neurological diseases. and comorbidity with somatic diseases [65,83], so the prevalence of FS in Uzbekistan is not known in exact numbers.

Paroxysms can be evaluated as FS, children's age also caused many conflicts. Currently, it is established that the diagnosis is valid when the age of children is determined from 6 months to 4 years (but 4-year-old children are not included in the category of early children, which some authors limit the periods of FS). A number of authors believe that FS can be recorded as a diagnosis in patients under 5 and even 6 years of age. The question of how to respond to various paroxysms of FS in children under 6 months of age is still not fully elucidated [5,29,69,84].

FS can be induced by both infectious and non-infectious causes [5,65]. Thus, any infectious disease can trigger FS. In children, 30-35% of cases of FS symptoms appearing for the first time in the first year of life are observed against the background of infections caused by human herpes virus type 6 (including roseola) [58,59,68,69]. Other viral diseases (influenza A, metapneumovirus, etc.) rarely provoke FS, in this regard, bacterial damage of the upper respiratory tract or acute gastroenteritis (especially Shigella caused by various pathogenic microorganisms) is of great importance [58]. In most cases, febrile seizures occur when the body temperature rises sharply to high numbers, which is associated with hypoxia of the brain. It is known that with an increase in body temperature of only 1 oC, the intensity of exchange processes in the brain increases by 7-10%, as a result, the need for oxygen increases. Seizures are significantly less likely to occur when the body temperature rises slowly, as there is time for cerebral blood flow to increase sufficiently to prevent hypoxia [67].

There are quite a few cases where the body temperature rises to febrile values, where the infection is not the cause. Non-infectious causes of FS include tooth eruption, endocrine, resorptive, psychogenic, reflex and central hyperthermia [17,31]. It is important to mention that increased FS or seizure readiness in children with cardiac disorders is considered to be the cause of secondary ischemic damage of MAT [102]. Among the various etiological factors of the development of seizures, the role of pathological course of pregnancy and childbirth is important. In this case, perinatal damage to the brain is of great importance in the occurrence and development of seizures [42,44]. Many studies have established the important role of metabolic genesis in the occurrence of seizures in early childhood. Hypocalcemia, hypomagnesemia, and hypoglycemia are known to be major metabolic causes [85,85,102]. The level of total calcium in the extracellular fluid, according to the literature, is in the range of 2.5-3.4 mmol/l, and the amount of ionized calcium is 45% of the total amount and varies in the range of 1.1-1.5 mmol/l.

Clinical signs of hypocalcemia appear when total calcium falls below 1.9 mmol/L. The treatment and prevention of hypocalcemia in children usually includes a number of correction mechanisms - stable interaction of the hormones of the parathyroid (parathyroid hormone - PTH) and thyroid (calcitonin - CT) glands, ensuring a stable normal concentration of calcium with the help of vitamin D metabolites [15].

In the pathogenesis of FS, the role of disturbances in the metabolism of some macro- and/or microelements is considered to be very important, as evidenced by studies focused on studying the neurophysiological functions of sodium, calcium, phosphorus and other elements. Currently, some disturbances in the metabolism of neurotransmitters (in particular, an increase in the level of neopetrin in the cerebrospinal fluid (CSF) and a decrease in the concentration of amino-fatty acids) are considered as one of the mechanisms important in the development of FS in children [19,90].

Sh.Sh. Shamansurov, together with co-authors, the results of the study of the dynamics of changes in the amount of $Ca2+$ in the blood serum of early-year-old children show that it is more important in febrile and afebrile seizures, especially in children with AFS, where gross and expressive neurological disorders, a large number of attacks and aggravation of seizures are noted, compared to the norm. came to the conclusion that it shows a significant decrease. Usually, the efficiency of the synaptic transmission of the nerve impulse is associated with changes in the extracellular fluid, high levels of calcium in the blood, changes in biochemical and biophysiological processes, in particular, in the processes that control the metabolic balance [85-87]. This, in turn, simultaneously causes an increase in the level of Ca in the cytoplasm, functional changes in the system of interneuronal connections, as well as changes in the electrical potentials of nerve cell membranes, which was confirmed in a number of studies [71].

FS occurs as a result of genetic predisposition, when the immature membrane of neurons is highly sensitive to the pathological effects of high temperature and responds to it with "failure" (disruption of structure and functional properties) [38,49,50]. Thus, if we exclude the genetic aspects of the disease described below, 2 main features should always be considered in FS: a low threshold of seizure activity and hyperthermia (fever) - a triggering factor of FS [31,46,146].

Returning to the aspects that distinguish true fever from hyperthermia, the temperature control center (its thermosensitive and temperature-determining areas) is located in the preoptic area of the anterior part of the hypothalamus, near the base of the third ventricle, and ensures that the "core" temperature is maintained within the appropriate limits, the body's functions related to heat production and heat production. we remember that it responds to management. The temperature control center maintains a balance between heat output and heat supply; at the same time, noradrenaline, 5-hydroxytryptamine, acetylcholine, prostaglandins, thyrotropic hormone (TTH) and possibly adrenocorticotropic hormone (ACTH) are involved in chemical neuromediation processes [18, 68].

Fever is caused by exogenous and endogenous pyrogens (exo and endotoxins); the other is lipopolysaccharide (LPS). When endotoxins enter the blood, they combine with a specific plasma protein, aFSer which the resulting complex interacts with the SD14 receptor on the macrophage membrane, during which many secondary endogenous pyrogens are released (interleukin-1 (IL-1), IL-6, IL-8, tumor necrosis factor (O'NO) (FNO)) [31]. Interleukins and O'NO enter the area of the circumventricular organ (OVLT), where they leave the vascular border, increase the synthesis of cyclooxygenase (TsOG) and lead to the formation of prostaglandins (PG)s. Lipophilic PG easily crosses the barrier between the OVLT and brain tissue and affects the temperature control center (increasing the "set point", which reduces heat input and increases heat output) [17,30,39].

This mechanism of FS development during fever does not always work, otherwise every child with a high temperature would have such a seizure. Hyperthermia usually leads to the development of seizures in the presence of preexisting perinatal pathology and genetic factors in the brain [17,29]. Decompensation occurs in children with MAT pathology, as a result of which the increase in temperature provokes seizures, because "a rapid (1 degree per hour) and extreme (up to 40-41 degrees) increase in body temperature leads to microcirculation disorders, metabolic disorders, and rapidly increasing dysfunction of vital organs and systems. followed by." [31].

Each age period has its own etiopathogenetic factors for the occurrence of seizure syndromes, in particular, FS. In the occurrence of this disease in children, perinatal factors, in particular cerebral hypoxia, developmental anomalies, genetic determination, as well as small metabolic shiFSs that occur in the children's body in one or other pathological conditions, which lead to seizure activity and brain excitability, anatomic-physiological peculiarities of the children's brain, play an important role. holds [5,15,35,43].

Thus, according to a number of studies, factors leading to the development of febrile seizures, genetic predisposition, especially FS in the anamnesis of close relatives, pre- and perinatal brain damage, discharge from the hospital in the neonatal period, 28 days of age or later, frequent occurrence of viral infections, high temperature, delay in psychomotor development [22,23,47]. In most cases, FS
in children develops aFSer receiving a vaccine, that is, as a postvaccine complication [5,6].

The study of the state of the autonomic nervous system in the periods between seizures in children with severe febrile seizures with the registration of all types of pathological activity: sharp waves in the composition of hypnogagic hypersynchronization, sleep exalter spindles, K-complexes revealed the presence of parasympathetictonia. Sympathotonia detected in children with simple and complex FS, when detected by EEG, was accompanied by sharp waves in both sleep excitatory spindles and K-complexes, which probably indicates a non-specialized process associated with the development of mechanisms that activate the antiepileptic systems of MAT. The presence of normotonia in some children with simple FS probably testifies to the fact that the process is of positive quality, with minimal changes in the EEG. Later, when patients with epilepsy were studied during periods between seizures, the following autonomic disturbances were revealed: an increase in parasympathetic activity in the right hemisphere and sympathetic activity in the leFS hemisphere, respectively.

In addition, as a result of studies conducted in patients with FS, high excretion of amines in children with FS, caused by genetic or perinatal pathology, based on dysfunction of the upper segments autonomic centers and primarily in the structures of the limbic-reticular complex, ergotropic (sympatho-adrenal) It was found that hypertonus is the consequence [52].

1.2. Genetic aspects of febrile seizures in children.

Currently, genetic, social, exo- and endogenous factors of febrile seizures are sufficiently studied. Many studies have investigated genetic predisposition to FS. The hypothesis that a genetic determinant of susceptibility to seizures is a consequence of a general defect in catecholamine metabolism in MAT has been widely accepted [80,87,137,169].

According to the data in the literature, 24% of children with FS have a family member who suffers from (or previously suffered from) a similar pathology in the family of the first consanguinity. Only 20% of patients have no family history of FS [118,128]. However, the presence of a genetic predisposition to FS leads to an increased risk of FS recurrence [109].

Although the presumed mode of inheritance of FS has not been clearly defined, it is highly likely that it is autosomal dominant or polygonal [146].

Currently, geneticists have identified a number of autosomal dominant genes responsible for the occurrence of febrile seizures. They are located on chromosomal loci: 5q14-15, 19r13.3, 19q, 8q13-q21, 2q23-34. A gene defect located on chromosome 19p is the result of a mutation of the sodium channel α-1 subunit SCN1B. Thus, a genetic predisposition in FS is supported by numerous observations and is well documented.

Japanese researchers also described phenotypic characteristics of patients with two recently described mutations of the α1 Na+ channel SCN1A gene subunit [128]. Mutations in this gene also cause FS Dravé syndrome, the onset of temporal lobe epilepsy [6,174]. Several genetic loci are recognized to associate susceptibility to FS. Duplication and deletion of segments of the SCN1A gene reduce Na+ channel function, de novo and can occur with amino acid substitutions in the gene [134,152]. According to Mulley (2013), in hereditary genetic determination, permeability disorders in neuronal membranes lead to afebrile seizures in 2-7% of patients, 3% of patients under the age of 7 develop epilepsy. Currently, the OMIM international database contains information on more than 10 types of FS with different gene loci [42,152,159,169].

1.3. Clinical signs and course of febrile seizures in children and ways to optimize their treatment.

FSs are divided into simple (typical) and complex (atypical) types according to their clinical features. In some studies, FS attacks are only generalized epileptic seizures (so-called "grandmal"), i.e. symmetrical tonic-clonic seizures in the arms and/or legs, but sometimes a focal component can be detected and classified as complex or atypical [5,10].

Typical FS is characterized by relatively short duration and general tonic-clonic character; in which the main indicators of the child's psychomotor development usually correspond to age norms [66], and changes in electroencephalography (EEG) are not observed or age-appropriate changes are noted [5,18,85]. Typical or simple FS is also called positive quality, because in the unrepeated state, it does not have a negative effect on the child's psycho-speech development. Atypical FS is characterized by a long duration (more than 15 minutes), generalization (with the possibility of a focal component) and lateralization of the attack, sometimes postictal hemiplegia occurs, and in the EEG study, focal changes are oFSen registered (probably typical epileptiform changes) [22,81, 90]. In addition, it can be said that typical FS has no evidence of organic lesions in MAT in the anamnesis, and atypical FS has a high frequency of perinatal damage to the nervous system and brain [86,90,102].

However, there are studies in the literature that show that the recurrence of FS does not depend on the type of FS [22]. In some cases, atypical FS reaches several hours in duration. As a result, transient postictal hemiplegia may develop (in 0.4% of cases).

FS lasting more than 30 minutes is oFSen recorded as "febrile status epilepticus" (ES) [31]. FS Dravé syndrome, a severe myoclonus-epilepsy of infancy occurring in the first year of life, was considered a condition of clinical onset. FS is observed in 14% of patients with late-onset cervical epilepsy - Gasto type [6].

Another condition commonly seen with FS is generalized epilepsy with febrile seizures plus (GEFS+), an autosomal dominant disorder characterized by more than 5 epilepsies. The listed type of FS epilepsy persists (recurring) even aFSer the patient is over 6 years old; GEFS+ is also associated with afebrile seizures [21,44,48,50]. Kitaeva V.E. reported a case of FIRES disease in school-age children, in which pharmacoresistant status epilepticus occurred for 2 weeks aFSer temperature elevation to high numbers [32].

Therefore, when studying children with FS, it is very important to correctly determine the main diagnosis, while conducting a differential diagnosis of the condition.

Data from the literature on the studies conducted confirm that typical FS does not have psycho-speech disorders. At the same time, it is important to mention that even one episode of FS occurs very oFSen in children who have experienced perinatal damage to the nervous system. We can certainly associate the delay in psycho-verbal development with PPNS in typical FS. Prolonged and repeated FS can lead to atrophy of the hippocampus, and an increase in the number of FS attacks can cause a delay in psycho-speech development and negatively affect the formation of cognitive status [28,30]. In most cases, children with FS have memory and attention deficits, as well as rapid fatigue in any type of physical and mental load, oFSen these are hyperactive emotionally labile children who are difficult to control and manage [12]. Early onset, multiple repetitions and long duration of FS affect not only the development of speech, the formation of auditory-speech memory, but also lead to motor side effects in these children [30].

1.4. Diagnosis, differential diagnosis of febrile seizures in children.

Usually, the diagnosis of FS is based on a careful collection of anamnesis, physical examination (somatic and neurological status), assessment of the level of psychomotor and emotional development, peculiarities of the seizure course and their frequency (duration, location, generality, lateralization, presence/absence of post-seizure hemiplegia, etc.). determined based on [46,47].

Laboratory and equipment methods are not necessary in determining the diagnosis of FS, because changes in indicators may be related to the underlying disease [5,6,69,70]. In particular, most neurologists consider it unnecessary to use neuroimaging methods (computerized tomography (CT) and/or magnetic resonance imaging (MRT) of the brain) aFSer the first attack of FS in children, sometimes parents demand additional research methods [5].

Electroencephalographic studies show characteristic (paroxysmal) changes in only 1.4–22% of children with FS, and are recommended to be performed at least 10 days aFSer the episode [51,86]. An EEG study is included in the examination protocol of patients with FS in most countries. In order to distinguish FS from the onset of epilepsy based on the results of the EEG examination of the brain, the time of FS occurrence, the period of examination depending on the age of the child are important. Some researchers [135,137,183] observe epileptiform changes in the EEG in children with FS, identifying it as a risk factor for the development of epilepsy in children. Some researchers [148,184] have identified epileptiform activity in the EEG in the form of focal slowing [22,23,51,86]. Epileptiform activity and slowing of background activity were observed in the EEG of the brains of more than half of the children with epilepsy, compared with the treated children.

In a number of cases, the results of biochemical research of blood should not be ignored, which allow to determine the amount of macro- and microelements (Sa, RO4, Mg, etc.) For this reason, it is necessary to consider the biochemical study of blood in children with FS as a necessary diagnostic measure that really helps in differentiating FS from other conditions [26,29,36].

As mentioned above, iron deficiency is one of the factors likely to lead to FS, therefore, it is necessary to carry out a complete blood test to detect iron deficiency anemia or hidden iron deficiency (general blood analysis, ferritin, etc.) [39,44].

It is necessary to distinguish true FS from other types of seizures occurring during fever, among such cases the following can be distinguished: 1) epileptic seizures caused by fever; 2) seizures in infectious diseases (meningitis, encephalitis) in MAT; 3) seizures associated with infectious diseases and, in their absence, metabolic disorders (hypoglycemia, hypocalcemia, hyponatremia, etc.) [25,26]. Seizures (and other paroxysms) on the background of high temperature in infants and children under 6 years of age are oFSen associated with neuroinfections and, of course, are not considered true FS [29,34].

1.5. diagnostic criteria for the transition of febrile seizures to afebrile.

In the literature, the problem of transition of FS to afebrile attacks is highlighted. According to researchers, the occurrence of at least one afebrile paroxysm in a child indicates the passing of an epileptic disease, that is, there is a possibility of epilepsy being diagnosed when there is a genetic predisposition to afebrile attacks [37,38]. This definition is ambiguous, because afebrile paroxysms, for example, caused by intoxications of various genesis, can be considered as a consequence of affective respiratory disorders [29]. The question of the correlation of FS with subsequent afebrile seizures and epilepsy remains controversial. According to epidemiological data, FS is the most common sign of predisposition to epilepsy in childhood, FS is detected in 15-25% of cases in the anamnesis of patients with epilepsy. In the anamnesis of children with FS, the rate of transition of FS to epilepsy does not exceed 2-10% [37]. Identifying the risk factors for the transition of FS to epilepsy determines the tactics of conducting patients with FS (the duration of observation, the size and number of conducted studies), as well as the need for the use of antiepileptic drugs.

FS occurs in 10-30% of many epileptic syndromes and at the onset of epilepsy, so 10-45% of patients with idiopathic focal epilepsy have an anamnesis, and 7% of children with rolandic epilepsy have relatives with FS. The maximum frequency of FS up to 30% is observed at the debut of positive-quality cervical epilepsy. In recent years, FS occurring as part of idiopathic focal epilepsy in infancy has been described. The frequency of FS in patients with positive-quality myoclonic epilepsy in infancy reaches 27%, it is less common in patients with the following forms of idiopathic generalized epilepsy: Dooze syndrome - 11%, absence epilepsy in adolescents - 12%, Tassinari syndrome - 15%, epilepsy with isolated generalized seizures. – 15%, myoclonic epilepsy in adolescence – in isolated cases. An early predictor of the transition of FS to idiopathic focal epilepsies can be the detection of positive quality epileptiform patterns on the EEG recorded during sleep, in these forms of epilepsy only typical FS is found, which are oFSen associated with sleep [5,6,68,109].

Many researchers [5,6,22,81,88,90] identify risk factors that may lead to later development of epilepsy in children with febrile seizures as follows:

- presence of epilepsy or epileptic attacks of parents during childhood;
- neurological pathology in the child before the appearance of febrile seizures;
- delay in mental development;
- focal seizures (predominance of seizures on one side of the body, dizziness, facial deformity, etc.);
- continuous seizures (lasting more than 15 minutes);
- the presence of repeated febrile seizures or other paroxysmal conditions (frequent tremors in sleep, night terrors, sleepwalking, fainting, etc.);
- pathological changes in the electroencephalogram (EEG) that persist for more than 7 days aFSer the attack;
- the child's age is less than 1 year or older than 5 years;
- appearance of attacks when the temperature drops.

When there are 2 or more risk factors, long-term treatment with antiepileptic drugs is usually prescribed.

1.6. Approaches to the treatment of febrile seizures in children.

The medical and social importance of treating FS in children and preventing its progression to afebrile seizures is determined by the increasing incidence of FS. However, for many pediatricians and neurologists who are faced with the problem of treating FS, important issues are: when to start treatment (aFSer the first, second, etc. attacks); duration of treatment; are possible consequences of treatment with anticonvulsants. For many years, the main problem of FS has been the question of the feasibility and extent of specialized treatment of this type of paroxysms in children. There is relative agreement on the treatment of FS attacks themselves, that is, when the disease is treated in the intensive care unit setting, in the acute phase, and cannot be delayed [2]. However, the management of children with febrile seizures and the long-term prevention of relapses, as well as the problem of antiepileptic drugs (AEDs) and the prevention of the transition of FS to afebrile manifestations, are still controversial and require new approaches [21,27 ,38].

Thus, the use of diazepam (seduxen, relanium, etc.) or phenobarbital (lorafene, merlit, etc.) is recommended almost everywhere, in many countries, to correct paroxysms triggered by an increase in body temperature to febrile values [36,44,50]. Diazepam is prescribed in the amount of 0.2–0.5 mg/kg of body weight, lorazepam – 0.005–0.02 mg/kg of body weight, and phenobarbital – in the amount of 3–5 mg/kg of body weight (daily dose) [36,37]. Foreign authors note the relatively high efficiency of diazepam prescribed at a dose of 0.33 mg/kg of body weight [48]. Abroad, the practice of prescribing diazepam in an enema (rectal) is widespread [50,74]. In the near future, valproate sodium is likely to be used parenterally for this purpose, but there is relatively little experience of its use in neuropediatrics [91].

Although reduction of hyperthermia to normal or subfebrile values does not guarantee prevention of recurrent seizures, normalization of high body temperature caused by FS in children is a generally recognized practice almost everywhere.

To reduce body temperature, physical cooling methods are widely recommended: wiping the body with water (cold or hot), wiping different parts of the body with an alcohol solution, undressing the child, airing the room (with the child), etc. [12,74]. Rather than using physical cooling methods, the use of antipyretic agents is considered appropriate [14,29]. Therefore, the appointment of drugs with antipyretic activity is indicated for children with FS.

In some countries, paracetamol, called acetaminophen (eng. - acetaminophen), inhibits PG synthesis and blocks both forms of cyclooxygenase (COG¬1 and COG¬2); In MAT, paracetamol affects temperature and pain control centers [88].

Paracetamol is used in a dose of 10-15 mg/kg of body weight per day (doses of rectal forms of paracetamol for children can reach 20 mg/kg of body weight per day).

Ibuprofen, along with paracetamol, has been relatively widely used as an antipyretic agent in recent years. Paracetamol can be used together with ibuprofen in FS. Ibuprofen is prescribed at the rate of 5–10 mg/kg of body weight (single dose), up to 4 times a day [18].

In children with FS, it is reasonable to try to lower the body temperature, even if it does not reach febrile values, keeping it in the subfebrile range (from 37.5 oC to 38 oC) [9,18,88].

The main tasks of the doctor are to correctly diagnose febrile seizures, to conduct additional examinations, to determine the indications for hospitalization, treatment and tactics to prevent repeated paroxysms. Errors in the diagnosis of FS, failure to assess the risk factors for their recurrence and transition to epilepsy, failure to hospitalize patients on time lead to late diagnosis of neuroinfections and special forms of epilepsy, and as a result, incorrect treatment. All this creates conditions for the formation of stable changes in the child's neuro-psychic development that lead to disability [46,48,50].

Febrile seizures in most cases have a positive prognosis. Most children who develop normally before the onset of febrile seizures do not suffer from mental or neurological development. The percentage of transition of febrile seizures to epilepsy is 2-10% in children with a history of febrile seizures. Factors such as familial predisposition to epilepsy, complex nature of febrile seizures, long-term seizures, neuropsychological disorders are believed to increase the risk of developing epilepsy from birth [63,68].

In the treatment of FS, it was noted by specialists that oFSen unfounded anticonvulsant therapy is prescribed by pediatricians and neurologists. The need for such therapy should always be justified. For many years, the main problem of FS has been the question of the feasibility and extent of specialized treatment of this type of paroxysms in children. Relative agreement is observed regarding the treatment of FS attacks. Thus, diazepam (seduxen, relanium), lorazepam (lorafene, merlit) or phenobarbital are recommended almost everywhere to correct paroxysms caused by an increase in body temperature to febrile values. Diazepam - 0.2-0.5 mg/kg (daily dose), lorazepam - 0.005-0.02 mg/kg, and phenobarbital - 3-5 mg/kg. Foreign experts note the relatively high efficiency of diazepam prescribed at a dose of 0.33 mg/kg. To reduce body temperature, physical cooling methods are widely used: wiping the body with water (cold or hot), wiping different areas of the body with an alcohol solution, undressing the child, airing the room (with the child), etc. [18,88].

Treatment and management of patients with FS receive considerable attention in the literature. According to the authors, complex therapy using nootropic drugs in young doses is recognized depending on the somatic condition of the body [5,15,36,37]. It is also very important to correct psycho-speech disorders in atypical FS. According to the authors of the study, the correction of mental and speech disorders should be implemented comprehensively [26,27,30,44,74,75]. It is necessary to include a course of drugs, training with a speech therapist and a speech therapist, as well as to correct the instability of micro- and macroelements [3,11,12,13,14,36,66]. Activities with children in a comfortable environment and in the form of games are recommended. It is very important for parents to communicate with their children, mostly in the same language, because this is one of the elements of correction [44,45]. In recent years, methods of stimulation therapy - micropolarization method, transcranial magnetic stimulation method have become very popular [34,44,45], which improves the effect of complex correction.

Febrile seizures (FS) is a condition that is not officially considered epilepsy, but usually attracts the attention of pediatric neurologists and epileptologists, because it can oFSen lead to the development of epilepsy and the formation of permanent mental and neurological deficits [9,14,90]. At the same time, the increase in body temperature is directly related to the somatic condition [9,14,93]. Atypical FS is characterized by psycho-speech disorders. Although FS is considered to be the most common neurological disorder in childhood, many aspects of this problem are still poorly understood and unresolved.

CHAPTER 2
MODERN APPROACHES TO EARLY DIAGNOSIS AND TREATMENT OF FEBRILE SEIZURES IN CHILDREN.
2.1. General description of children with febrile seizures by gender and age

Clinical characteristics of febrile seizures, risk factors for their recurrence and afebrile transition, 60 subjects (35) with febrile seizures aged 6 months to 5 years (mean age 3.4±1.15) and meeting the study inclusion criteria were studied in the neurology department. a group of children (one boy and 25 girls) was separated. We divided this group of patients into 3 subgroups according to the nature of febrile seizures: subgroup 1 - with typical febrile seizures, 20 patients (6 girls and 14 boys) aged 6 months to 5 years (average age 3.0±1.17) children) child; Subgroup 2 - 20 children (8 girls and 12 boys) aged 6 months to 5 years (average age 3.2±1.06) with atypical febrile seizures; Subgroup 3 - 20 (8 girls and 12 boys) children aged 6 months to 5 years (average age 4±1.03) with afebrile seizures.

In order to complete the registration, the author of the study developed questionnaire No. 1 (Appendix 1). Perinatal anamnesis data, genetic factors (presence of febrile seizures, epilepsy in relatives); conditions under which seizures occurred (fever, temperature rise, type of background disease, frequency of diseases), information on the nature, frequency, duration of febrile seizures, information on neurological status, information on additional research methods (EEG, EEG-video-monitoring, CTG, MRI) entered.

Diagnosis of seizures in children was carried out according to the criteria recommended in the International Classification of Epilepsy and Epileptic Syndromes (1989).

The second stage: study of 60 patients aged 6 to 12 years (mean age 11.6±2.35) with a history of febrile seizures under the observation of a neurologist. Clinical, electroencephalographic, neuroradiological examinations were carried out in ambulatory conditions. We divided this group of patients into 2 subgroups according to the nature of febrile seizures: subgroup 1 – 30 children aged 6 to 12 years (mean age 1.11±2.44) who ended with FS epilepsy; In subgroup 2 - 30 children (10 girls and 20 boys) aged 6 to 12 years (average age 12.07±2.18) with atypical febrile seizures;

For this stage of the work, the author proposed the 2nd questionnaire (Appendix 2). It includes perinatal anamnesis data, genetic factors (presence of febrile seizures, epilepsies in relatives), conditions of occurrence of seizures (fever, temperature, type of background disease, frequency of diseases), information on the nature, frequency, duration of febrile seizures, treatment with anticonvulsant drugs. data, neurological status, data of additional research methods (EEG, EEG - video-monitoring, CTG, MRI) were entered.

In examined children, ENT organs: tonsillitis (25%), rhinosinusitis (19%), nasopharyngeal pathology - 10.8%, hepatobiliary systems: biliary tract dyskinesia (59.2%), cholecystitis (18.3%), in the gastrointestinal tract: comorbidities were detected in the form of pathologies of keys (19.2%), anemias (32.5%), the following diseases experienced as a result of the collection of anamnesis were determined: viral hepatitis A (11.7%), childhood infections (76, 7%). In the studied children, frequent cases of ARVI (98.3%) and colds were observed, the number of episodes in the cold season was 3 times and more, which testifies to a significant decrease in the immune status.

2.2. Electroencephalography.

EEG was recorded using a 16-channel electroencephalograph "Neurokartograf-1-MBN" with spectral mapping of the "MBN" scientific-medical company (produced in 2003) with a time constant of 0.3 seconds. speed of "paper movement" - 30 mm/second. The value of the high-frequency filters is 30 Hz, the resistance of the electrodes is at most 10 kOhm. The sensitivity of the channels was 1 μV/mm. The calibration signal was equal to 50 μV, and the amplitude was equal to 50 mW. All studies were conducted in a darkened, noise-protected room, with the child sitting in a special chair or in the mother's arms. KEEG was obtained in the morning, mainly during physiological sleep, rarely during wakefulness. The occurrence of drowsiness was monitored by behavioral criteria (prolonged closing of the eyes) and autonomic indicators (decreased heart rate and muscle tone). Monopolar recording was performed using Neuro soFSware.

The process of placing the electrodes, the way they were placed on the child's head, corresponded to the international standard scheme "10-20%". KEEG recording was carried out unipolar, from eight symmetrical points of the shell: forehead (FsFd), central (CsCd), top of the skull (PsPd) and occiput (OsOd). As an indifferent, a special ear electrode worn on the child's ear was used. The electrodes were attached to the head using a soFS rubber helmet. KEEG was recorded in bipolar outputs. Age-related characteristics of bioelectrical activity in children's brains were taken into account in KEEG analysis. The definition of KEEG rhythmic activity was made on the basis of three criteria of rhythm identification: frequency range, tomographic location of the focus of activity, relation of rhythmic oscillations with movements (functional reactivity). Interpretation of KEEG data was carried out according to generally recognized criteria, taking into account the specific characteristics of age. Electroencephalograms made it possible to obtain an objective assessment of the state of bioelectrical activity of the brain in examined patients.

2.3. Magnetic resonance imaging.

For diagnostic purposes, magnetic resonance imaging (MRT) was performed (nuclear magnetic resonance - YaMR), which allows obtaining a detailed anatomical image of the head and spinal cord in different planes and at different levels based on the use of a magnetic field.

Magnetic resonance imaging is a highly effective, harmless and non-invasive diagnostic method, based on the specific arrangement of water between the layers of the myelin sheath due to the peculiarities of the protein-lipid structure of myelin membranes. This order is disrupted in demyelination, when some of the water is free. Due to the long-term relaxation of water in the magnetic field, areas of demyelination are defined as low-dense areas on T1-weighted images and high-dense areas on T2-weighted images.

MR-tomography magnetic field loading was carried out at 1.5 T, on the "" device of the Siemens company. The standard package of used pulse sequences included waist echo (640/15 msec) in T1 mode and T2 mode (4500/80msec), FLAIR - inversion-recovery and diffuse-suspension images in free water pressure mode. More attention was paid to axial and frontal projections. The maximum thickness of the section and the step of the tomograph is 4-10 mm. Children up to 6 months of age were examined mainly during physiological sleep, in a tightly wrapped position, aFSer breastfeeding. Examination of older children required the use of anesthesia to reduce the child's movements in order to avoid deterioration of MRI quality due to motion artifacts.

2.4. Complex neuropsychological research methods

Based on the neuropsychological test, L.I. Wasserman, E.D. Chomska, L.S. Tsvetkova, A.B. Partially modified using the methods of Semenovich [8, 64, 82], A.R. A traditional battery of Luria [40, 41] tests was obtained.

The neuropsychological method was adapted to the age of each patient. The main feature of the neuropsychological test was the age-appropriate use of methods, division and scoring of the patients.

The study relied on the existing traditional scheme of complex neuropsychological research. Sensitization conditions and loads were added to the structure of the study, including: "deaf manual", monomanual use of graphic tests (separately with the right and leFS hand), exclusion of auditory and speech control (closing eyes, biting the tongue), increasing the time and speed of experimental tests" enters.

To analyze the obtained data, A.R. The scoring system developed at the INX RAMN neuropsychological laboratory named afSer Burdenko under Lury's guidance was used:

"0 point" patient was allowed to perform the proposed experimental program without additional explanations;

"1 point" - given when small errors were observed that the patient corrected independently, almost without the participation of the experimenter;

"2 points" - given when the patient was able to perform tasks in several attempts, aFSer open instructions and guiding questions;

"3 points" - given when the experimenter was unable to perform the task many times, even aFSer detailed explanation.

1. Study of functional asymmetry of the brain.

Annette questionnaire, clapping, turning the clock, scratching, drawing vertical lines with the right and leFS hands on two sheets of paper (for children aged 11), jumping on one leg, putting one foot on the other, winking, eye blink test, clock test, " whisper" test.

2. Learning the field of actions

In the general description of the child's actions, it began with the study of disorders or retention. Attention was paid to general movements, gait stability or instability, movement control, speed, fluency, modification, rhythm. Subject-domestic and subject-play skills were studied in children of primary and secondary school age: child's actions in the form of play activities with objects; voluntary actions with objects according to speech instructions "catch the ball", "take the pen", "look at the window"; actions without speech guidance for imitation. Then the various manifestations of praxis were explored.

When studying clinical praxis, finger counting, "playing the grand piano", "fist-side-palm" tests, Ozeretsky test for reciprocal hand control (from 12 years old), reciprocal tapping, "Wall" graphic test, oral praxis tests were used.

When studying kinesthetic praxis, proxy of poses according to a visual pattern, proxy of poses according to a kinesthetic pattern, changing of poses according to a kinesthetic pattern, oral praxis were performed.

Then spatial and constructive praxis were studied using the following methods: Denmann test (repetition of shapes with right and leFS hand), Taylor and Rey-Osterritza tests, reflection of spatial images according to speech instructions, Benton, Heda test.

At the end of the movement domain studies, tests were used to evaluate complex movement programs.

3. To study the various manifestations of Gnosis.

First, visual-predlscht and spatial vision gnosis using right and leFS hand pointing, pointing to parts of one's body and face, Heda pattern (visual and spoken), visual object recognition, Poppelreiter test (recognition of erased/crossed images) was studied. Color gnosis: Primary color discrimination was assessed using color sequence repetition tests. Acoustic gnosis: location of sound distribution in space, assessment of sound rhythms, studied using repetition tests. Cutaneous-kinesthetic gnosis: discrimination of hand touch, Ferster's test (dermolection), kinesthetic sensation retention test, finger imitation methods were evaluated. Numerical gnosis and counting were then assessed using: superimposed, mirrored, deleted number recognition, simple counting, automated counting, and serial counting samples. Letter gnosis and reading: finding letters among similar letters, familiarizing letters in opposite and reverse positions, reading sentences written in different fonts, and oral reading of syllables and pseudowords were assessed. Writing was assessed at the end of this unit, using a sample copy of letters (printed, cursive, cursive).

4. Learning memory.

General memory was assessed by recounting everyday events and past events. Auditory-speech memory: repeating a series of words, "Triple" test, remembering and repeating sentences: direct; aFSer a late, empty pause; aFSer a pause filled with conversation (homogeneous interference); aFSer a pause (heterogeneous interference), memorization curve (6-10 words), simile and mental memory test, filled with the execution of different movement programs. Visual-object memory: remembering object images, symbolic forms.

5. The study of attention.

Burdon's correction test, Münsterber's test, Schulte's table.

6. Study of speech and speech processes

The examination of the speech began when he started communicating with the patient. The general communicative function of speech was studied: understanding of focused speech and non-verbal means - gestures, facial expressions, intonation, sharp oral and dialogic speech, automated, non-automated, phonemic discrimination test, spelling fluency test, forming adjectives, repeating rapid utterances, elementary school age assessment of sound pronunciation in children, sound analysis and synthesis, filling in linguistic material.

7. Study of mental processes

Visual-figurative, verbal-logical thinking was studied. Tests were used to understand the essence of the text, retelling, understanding the figurative meaning of proverbs, choosing verbal analogies, extracting redundant elements, limited flow of analogies, anagrams, understanding inflectional relations, understanding the structure of demonstrative agreement, understanding inverted constructions, understanding spatial relationships, understanding comparative constructions, discursive thinking: continuation of a series of numbers, completion of mathematical material, understanding of the conditions of the task was checked. 8. Study of the emotional sphere

The following methods were used: pictures, perception and assessment of the emotional content of the situation, study of the feeling of empathy, connection of the emotional state with facial expressions, expression of emotions (non-verbal behavior).

Abroad, the Denver Developmental Screening Test (DDST, 1990) is used as a screening test for patients aged 2 weeks to 6 years.

To standardize character testing, it is necessary to use test administration guidelines. It is allowed to estimate the number of indicators (marked with the symbol R) from the words of the parents. For each sub-level, the researcher should obtain at least three completed and three uncompleted tasks closest to the child's age. If the child fails to complete the task performed by 90% of his peers, then the answer is evaluated as "negative". If the child performs a task performed by less than 25% of his peers, then the response is evaluated as "progressive".

The following test options are possible:

1. Advancement of psychomotor development:

1.1. if the child received a response of 2 or more "improving" on any two or more items within the four assessment subscales;

1.2. if there are 2 "progressing" responses on one subscale, 1 "progressing" response on another, and no "negative" responses on the same subscale.

2. Delay in psychomotor development:

2.1. if the child received 2 or more "negative" answers on any two or more items within the four assessment subscales;

2.2. if there are no 2 "negative" responses in one sublevel, 1 "negative" response in another, and no "progressive" responses in the same sublevel.

3. Moderate or predictable delay:

3.1. if the child has 2 or more "negative" answers in one of the four subscales;

3.2. if one "negative" response is received in any of the four sublevels and there is no "progressive" response in that sublevel.

4. If the test results do not belong to the previous categories, in accordance with psychomotor development, appropriate for age

It is necessary to pay attention to some inconsistencies of the terms of acquisition of certain skills with the standards adopted in our country, which are oFSen associated with incorrect translation of the described skills and having two different meanings. The non-grouping of the examined signs according to the age ranges accepted in our country makes it difficult to unify the obtained results.

The Wechsler Intelligence Scale for Children is an individual test and is used for research and practical purposes to measure general cognitive abilities in children aged 5 to 15 years and 11 months. The test takes an average of 60-90 minutes and is conducted individually with a psychologist. The total value of the Vexlar intelligence scale ranges from 40 to 160 points (average – 100 points, standard deviation 15 points). The Wechsler intelligence test for children consists of 12 subtests, divided into two groups combining verbal and nonverbal subtests, respectively. Verbal subtests – to assess verbal-logical intelligence. Small tests allow to assess general development and the level and quality of knowledge. Small test: measures general awareness, ability to draw conclusions and generalizations, vocabulary, mathematical and logical abilities, memory capacity.

Nonverbal subtests are used to assess receptive characteristics that are less related to knowledge level. Nonverbal indicator: evaluates spatial thinking, assembly of parts, analytical-synthetic abilities, attention ability.

In the methodological instructions, sub-tests from 1 to 12 are presented sequentially, first all verbal, then non-verbal tests. However, the practice of using the Wechsler test has shown that it is better to mix verbal tests with non-verbal tests. Despite the fact that the test covers a large age group (from 5 years to 15 years and 11 months), the results start to look really informative and reliable from 7-8 years old.

Statistical methods. Descriptive statistics, selective comparison and correlation search, spatial data visualization methods were used during the statistical analysis of the data.

Mean values with 95% confidence interval (95% II) calculated by Klopper-Pearson method for quantitative indicators, absolute (units) and relative (in %) frequencies with exact 95% II were calculated for qualitative indicators. The analysis of the distribution of indicators included the construction of histograms of distributions and the separation of a mixture of distributions using the EM-algorithm.

Quantitative comparisons of groups were performed using the t-test in the case of 2 groups and one-way analysis of variance (ANOVA) in the case of 3 groups. When comparing groups on qualitative measures, data were entered into correlation tables, which were analyzed using the criterion of validity ratio (chi-square of maximum validity, $x^{\wedge}$) (Armitage et. al., 2002). Statistical significance was assessed using a Monte Carlo randomized procedure in the Cytel Studio StatXact (version 7.0; Cytel SoFSware Corporation, COA) package when cells were not filled in the correlation table (minimum expectation less than 5). Freeman–Tukey FS was calculated to search the cells of the correlation table, providing the statistical significance of the considered effects, and their statistical significance was evaluated (Sokal, Rohlf, 1995).

In order to search for predictors of the transition of FS to afebrile/epilepsy and to create risk models for its development, indicators were selected, according to which the strongest and statistically significant differences were found during the comparison. These indicators were then entered into a multiple logistic regression (Lang, 2011) model. The diagnostic performance of the obtained models was evaluated by sensitivity, specificity indicators, as well as the area of the descriptive ROC-curve constructed on the prediction result (Appendix 4). Calculations were performed in the MedCalc (v. 12.2.1; MedCalc SoFSware, Belgium) package.

CHAPTER 3.
RISK FACTORS FOR THE DEVELOPMENT OF FEBRILE AND AFEBRILE SEIZURES IN CHILDREN. CLINICAL COURSE, DIAGNOSIS AND COMPARATIVE DIAGNOSIS OF FEBRILE AND AFEBRILE SEIZURES.

3.1. Etiological, clinical-neurological and neurophysiological characteristics of febrile and afebrile seizures.

To study the clinical characteristics of febrile seizures, their recurrence and the risk factors for transition to a febrile form, from 01.01.2016 to 01.01.2021, who were treated in the neurology department and met the criteria for inclusion in the study, aged 6 months to 5 years (average age 3.4±1.15), a group consisting of 60 (35 boys and 25 girls) children with febrile seizures was divided. We divided this group of patients into 3 subgroups according to the nature of febrile seizures: Subgroup 1 - 20 patients (6 girls and 14 boys) aged 6 months to 5 years (mean age 3.0±1.17) with typical febrile seizures) child; Subgroup 2 - 20 children (8 girls and 12 boys) aged 6 months to 5 years (average age 3.2±1.06) with atypical febrile seizures; Subgroup 3 - 20 (8 girls and 12 boys) children aged 6 months to 5 years (average age 4±1.03) with afebrile seizures. Among the children examined in the main group, mainly 2-3-year-old children were noted. Thus, for example, about 55% of children with typical febrile seizures, and 65% of children in the group with ATFS, were in this age group. However, in the group with afebrile seizures, on the contrary, 4-5-year-old children prevailed (70%), while in the groups with TFS and ATFS, their number was 45% and 30%, respectively. The smallest group was children under 1 year old, in which 1 child was examined (3.3%).

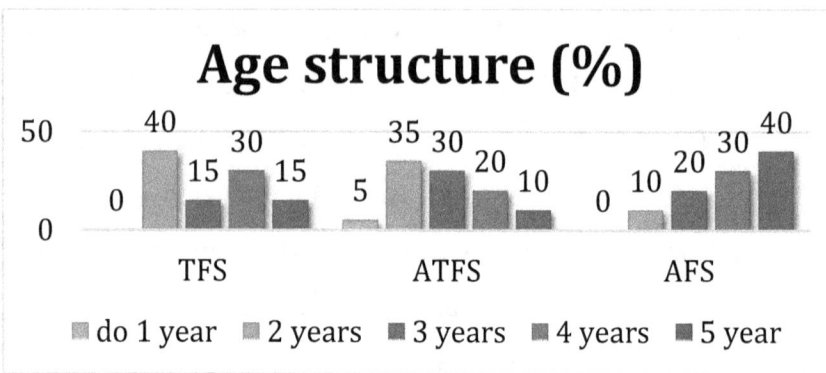

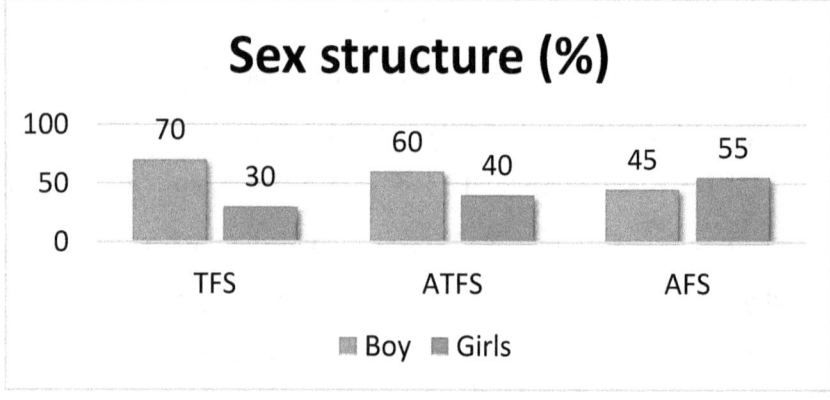

Figure 3.1 Distribution of children with febrile and afebrile seizures by age and sex.

Among examined children with febrile seizures, males predominated - 70% and 60% in TFS and ATFS subgroups, respectively. In the afebrile group, girls slightly predominated (55%).

Fever is one of the main conditions for the occurrence of febrile seizures. We analyzed the individual temperature characteristics associated with the onset of febrile seizures: the temperature level at the onset of seizures, the presence of fever before the onset of seizures, the rate of temperature increase at the onset of seizures.

Table 3.1

FS and AFS are the rate of temperature increase at the beginning of seizures.

	TFS		ATFS		AFS	
	H 20	%	H 20	%	H 20	%
The temperature at which seizures occur						
up to 38.0°C	6	30	3	15	3	15
Above 38.0°C	14	70	17	85	17	85
Occurrence of seizures						
When the temperature rises sharply	12	60	11	55	11	55
Not important	8	40	9	45	9	45

From the given data, it can be seen that febrile seizures in all groups oFSen occurred when the temperature was higher than 38.0 oC, while 30% of children in the TFS group had FS at a temperature of 38.0 oC, while in the ATFS and AFS groups, this figure was equal to 15%.

Seizures were the first sign of febrile illness in 10% of patients, and 90% of children were previously ill and febrile. In more than 50% of patients in each subgroup, FS oFSen occurred during a rapid increase in temperature.

Genetic factors are of great importance in the development of febrile seizures. We determined the presence of febrile seizures/epilepsy and the frequency of febrile seizures among relatives of children with febrile seizures and epilepsy to determine genetic predisposition.

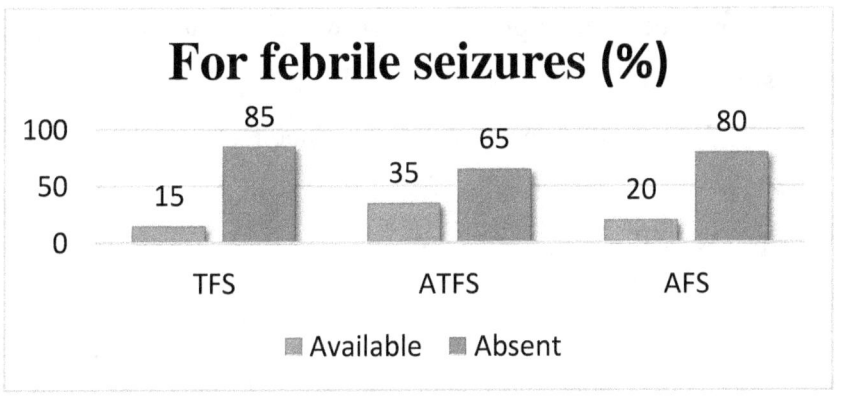

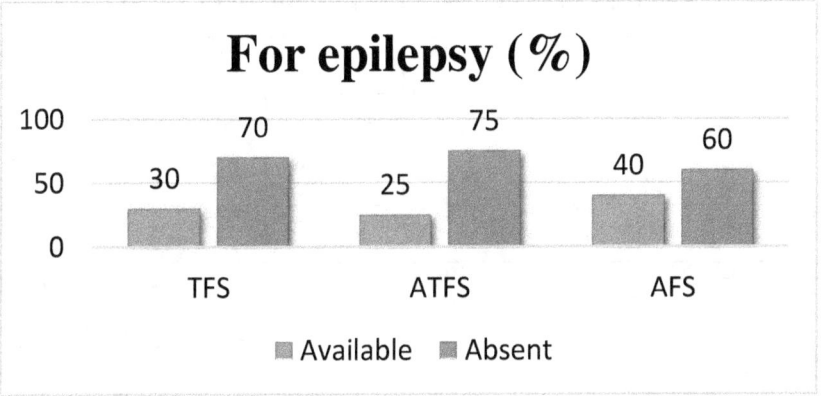

Figure 3.2 State of FS and AFS genetic predisposition.

Hereditary predisposition to febrile seizures was most oFSen observed in the ATFS group (35%), while in the AFS and TFS groups, this indicator was 20% and 15%, respectively. As for the level of kinship, the genetic predisposition was mainly found in the first family relatives. Hereditary predisposition to afebrile seizures was found more in the AFS group (40%), while in the ATFS and TFS groups, this figure was 25% and 30%, respectively. As for the level of kinship, in this case, the genetic predisposition was also determined in the first family relatives.

Factors that increase the likelihood of febrile seizures include perinatal pathology, which can affect the clinical course of FS, as well as their outcome.

Table 3.2

Factors that increase the likelihood of FS and AFS.

	TFS		ATFS		AFS	
	N 20	%	N 20	%	N 20	%
The passage of pregnancy						
Positive	12	60	9	45	5	25
Negative	8	40	11	55	15	75
Gestosis	8	40	8	40	10	50
Risk of miscarriage	0	0	3	15	5	25
СФПЕ	0	0	0	0	3	15
Birth						
In due course	14	7	15	7	13	6

		0		5		5
Weakness of reproductive activity	3	15	2	10	4	20
Before the deadline		0	2	10	2	10
Caesarean section	3	15	1	5	1	5
Weight at birth, g						
2500-4500	15	75	14	70	14	70
Less than 2500	3	15	3	15	4	20
More than 4500	2	10	3	15	2	10

We studied the immediate intranatal period during pregnancy (pregnancy, the risk of termination of pregnancy and the presence of chronic fetoplacental insufficiency) and the weakness of labor, preterm labor and surgical delivery.

The negative course of pregnancy was observed more in patients with afebrile seizures - 75%, in which mothers were most oFSen diagnosed with gestosis (50%), while the risk of termination of pregnancy was noted in 25% of mothers: in patients with ATFS, the disorder of the course of pregnancy was in 55% of mothers, with predominance of gestosis in 40% in children, the risk of miscarriage was found in 15% of cases. Pregnancy pathology was the least detected in children with FS (in 40% of cases), and all of them were manifested by gestosis. It should be mentioned that chronic fetoplacental insufficiency was found only in patients with AFS (15%).

As for the intranatal period, in this case, in 70% of the patients we examined, the deliveries were physiological, on time. Poor fertility was more common, but no significant differences were found between the groups. Birth weight varied between 2.5 kg and 4.5 kg in 71.7% of patients. About 16.7% of all children were born underweight, and 11.6% were born overweight.

Fever, which causes febrile seizures, is oFSen caused by acute infectious diseases: ARVI, otitis media, pneumonia, intestinal infections, inflammation of the urinary tract.

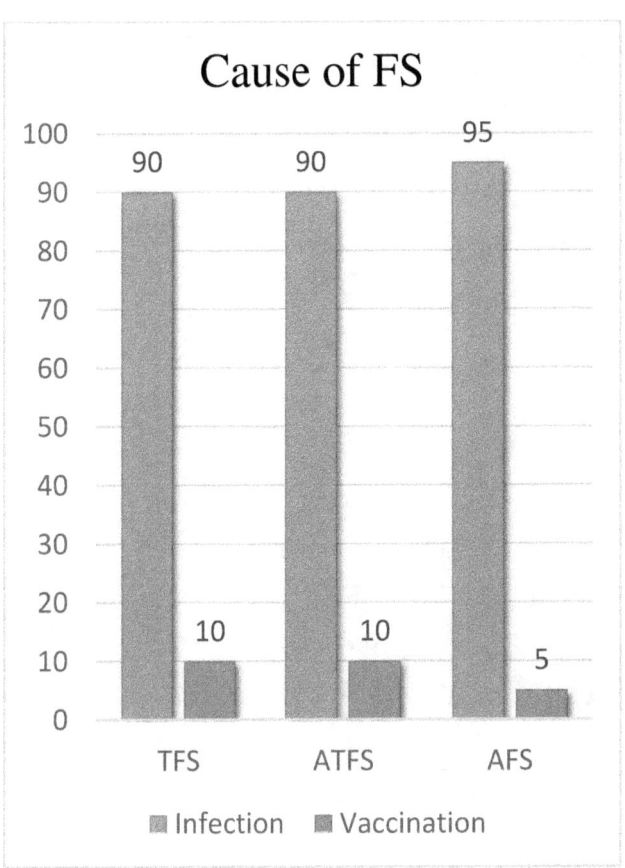

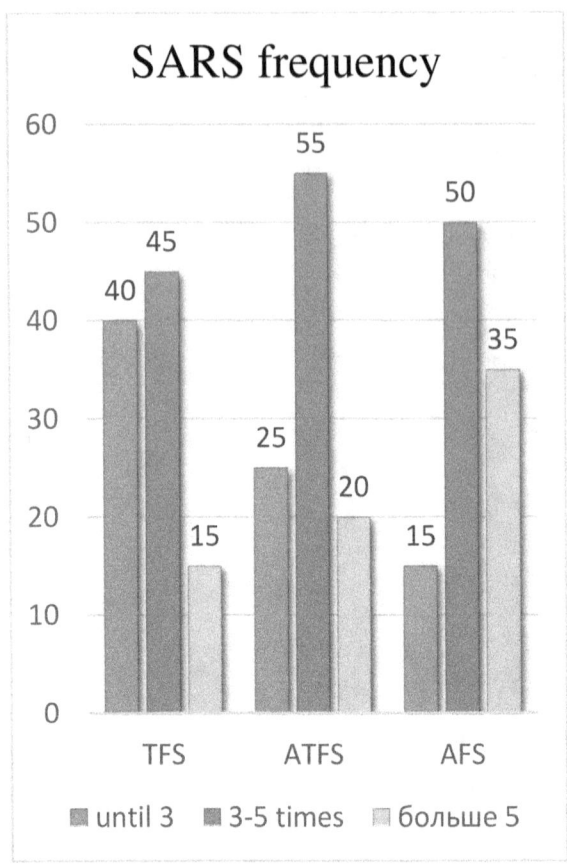

Figure 3.3 Background diseases and vaccination in children with febrile seizures.

These infections are the cause of most childhood seizures. Also, a febrile reaction to vaccination can be considered a cause of FS. In our study, the main reason for the occurrence of FS in children was the presence of an infectious process - 88.3%, and the reason for the increase in febrile seizures during vaccination was acute respiratory infection in most cases (88.7%), the number of children who experienced seizures aFSer vaccination - 7 (11.3%) made it.

However, it should be noted that the frequency of occurrence of infectious diseases affected the probability of occurrence of seizures. So, for example, most of the children we examined were frequent patients, patients with infectious diseases more than 3 times a year.

We analyzed the characteristics of febrile seizures in children.

3.3 Schedule

Analysis of specific characteristics of febrile seizures in children.

	TFS		ATFS		AFS	
	N 20	%	N 20	%	N 20	%
FS debut						
Up to one year old	6	30	5	25	4	20
1-3 years old	11	55	14	70	16	80
3-5 yers old	3	15	1	5	0	0
The nature of the FS attack						
Generalized	20	100	16	80	12	60
Focal	0	0	4	20	8	40
The nature of an AFS attack						
Generalized		0		0	12	60
Focal		0		0	8	40

In 68.3% of the patients we examined, the onset of febrile seizures corresponded to 1-3 years of age, in 25% of patients, febrile seizures began before the age of one year, and in only 6.7% of patients, FS began aFSer 3 years of age. In the AFS group, seizures did not start aFSer 3 years of age. 30% of children in the TFS-observed group had FS before 1 year of age.

In most children (90%), seizures had a general appearance. Of these, 63.3% of children had general tonic-clonic seizures and 13.3% had clinical seizures, 10% of patients had seizures that started with weakness. All attacks were characterized by a sudden and complete loss of consciousness. A tonic spasm with an upward movement of the eyelids, followed by clonic tremors in the limbs, facial muscles, breath holding, and cyanosis of the nose-lip triangle became characteristic of a general tonic-clonic attack. Seizure duration was usually up to 5 minutes, and the post-seizure period was characterized by weakness, mild loss of consciousness, and post-seizure sleep.

As for focal seizures, they were most oFSen noted in the AFS observed group and accounted for 40% of the examined children in the group. In comparison, in the group with ATFS, only 4 (20%) children had focal different seizures, whereas in the group with typical FS, no such seizures were observed. These attacks began with a focal component, and then passed to a secondary-general appearance. Basically, the focal component was imperceptible to parents, it was noted only when we identified complaints.

The study of the neurological condition was carried out in the traditional way. During the examination, disorders in the neurological status were found in 70% of the examined children. Disturbances in neurostatus were found more oFSen in the AFS and ATFS groups (80% and 75%, respectively), in the TFS observed group, focal symptoms were found in more than half of the patients.

OFSen, during the evaluation of the neurological status in typical febrile seizures, diffuse small foci symptomatology was detected in 8 (40%) children in the form of autonomic disorders, which were manifested in the form of profuse sweating and discoloration of the skin. In 6 (25%) children, increased alertness and tendon reflexes were observed. In the form of flattening of the nasolabial fold and facial asymmetry, disorders in the brain were detected a little less - in 15% of the examined children. Delay in speech and psycho-speech development was observed in 20% of patients.

3.4 Schedule

Assessment of neurological status in febrile seizures.

	TFS		ATFS		AFS	
	N=20	%	N=20	%	N=20	%

Neurostatus						
Without changes	9	45	5	25	4	20
With changes	11	55	15	75	16	80
Eye movement disorder		0		0	3	15
Ptosis		0		0	1	5
Let's complain		0	2	10	3	15
Nystagmus		0	3	15	3	15
Facial asymmetry	2	10	5	25	8	40
Smoothness of the nasolabial fold	3	15	2	10	9	45
Bulbar disorders		0		0	1	5
Dysarthria		0	2	10	7	35
Hyperkinesis		0		0	6	30
Movement control disorder		0	2	10	4	20
Increases and revitalization of ankle reflexes	5	25	7	35	13	65
Pathological reflexes		0		0	3	15
Vegetative dysfunction	8	4	11	5	12	6

		0		5		0

Children in the group with atypical febrile attacks also complained of more impaired autonomic functions (in 55% of cases). 40% of children had disturbances in the reflex field. In this group of patients, pathology of the facial nerve was added, as well as eye movement disorders in the form of squint (10%) and nystagmus (15%), bulbar disorders in the form of dysarthria (10%), and discoordinating disorders were noted in 10% of patients. Delay in speech and psycho-speech development was noted in 25% of children.

Most oFSen, neurostatus disorders were detected in the group of children with afebrile seizures. As in the above-mentioned groups, vegetative dysfunction and disturbances in the reflex field were found in children (60% and 65%, respectively, but the delay in speech and psycho-speech development came to the fore in this group, which was observed in 80% of children. Also, facial asymmetry in children of this group (40% of children) and smoothing of the nasolabial fold (45% of subjects) facial nerve pathologies, as well as eye movement disorders in the form of squint (15%), nystagmus (15%) and ptosis (5%) and dysarthria (35%) to bulbar disorders, hyperkinesis (30% of examined children) and pathological reflexes (15%) were added, coordination disorders were noted in 15% of children.

Hardware inspection methods

We performed an EEG study of the brain, which was usually performed at least 10 days aFSer the seizure. In our work, the visual analysis of EEG was carried out in a generally accepted way, taking into account age.

In general, the bioelectric pace in most children reflected a change in the character of the whole brain in the form of disturbances in the formation of age-related bioelectric activity.

According to the results of visual evaluation of electroencephalograms, traces of bioelectrical activity in the brain were detected in 40% of the examined children, in most cases it was noted in the group with afebrile seizures (45% of children), while in the TFS and ATFS groups, these disorders occurred in 35% and 40% of children, respectively. met

58.3% of children had alpha rhythm instability. It was recorded in 55% of children with TFS, in more than half of children with ATFS, and in 70% of children with afebrile seizures.

Hypersynchronization was also found in 20% of those examined, in which alpha-activity spread from the occipital area to the frontal cortex areas of the brain. Basically, hypersynchronization was found in patients with afebrile seizures, while in the ATFS group they were observed in only 10% of children, while in the group of typical febrile seizures, such disorders were not observed.

3.5 Schedule

Results of FS and AFS hardware inspection methods.

	TFS		ATFS		AFS	
	N=20	%	N=20	%	N=20	%
MPT						
Without pathology	20	100	17	85	15	75
Pathology	0	0	3	15	5	25
Moderate expansion of the leFS ventricle, acute expansion of the right ventricle. BSG indirect signs.		0		1	5	1	5
The rate of encephalopathy in the vein		0		0		0
signs of "brain immaturity", delayed myelination		0	2	10	1	5
Atrophic process expressed in the areas of the forehead		0		0		0
Focal density changes in brain matter		0		0	2	10
Callous body agenesis, transparent barrier cyst		0		0	3	15

Arachnoid cyst of the brain		0		0	1	5
EEG						
BEA derailment	7	35	8	40	9	45
Alpha-rhythm instability	11	55	10	50	14	70
Hypersynchronization		0	2	10	10	50

No abnormalities were found when alpha rhythm was evaluated in patients with FS. The average alpha rhythm in patients was 82.14 ±16.1 μV (98 μV and more - 36%, less than 19 μV - 6%).

In patients with afebrile seizures, an insignificant level of epiactivity was also noted, which was mainly observed in the occipito-occipital region of the brain - in 25% of the examined children, and slightly less in the central-temporal regions of the brain - in 15% of cases, and in 10% of cases EA was observed in the frontal areas of the cerebral cortex. marked.

The presence of more slow waves, added and sharp waves in the EEG image was observed in 28.3% of patients, dysfunction of trunk structures was observed in 18.3% of children, and diffuse widespread discharges of sharp waves could be observed in 11.7% of children. Focal epileptiform activity was observed in 2 (10%) patients with afebrile seizures.

It should be mentioned that aFSer repeated EEG, epiactivity was not observed in only one patient, and epileptiform activity was again detected in another EEG study.

Magnetic resonance imaging of the brain was performed mainly according to indications, for example, in atypical febrile seizures or in the development of organic lesions of the nervous system. In some cases, MRT was conducted at the decision of the parents.

In the group of patients with ATFS, only 15% of children had changes in the MRI image of the brain, which were manifested by "brain immaturity" and delayed myelination and moderate enlargement of the lateral ventricles.

In the group with AFS, changes in the rate of neuroimaging were observed slightly more (25% of children), and the nature of the damage was more extensive. To the above-mentioned signs such as "brain immaturity" (5%) and enlargement of the lateral ventricles (5%), as well as focal changes (10% of children) and agenesis of the corpus callosum with a cyst of the transparent wall (15%) were added. A GM arachnoid cyst was also found in one child.

Chapter 3 Conclusions

Thus, when we studied children with febrile and afebrile seizures, it was found that FS was more oFSen observed in 2- and 3-year-old children (55%), while in the group of children with AFS, on the contrary, 4- and 5-year-old patients were the majority - 70%. When gender differences were analyzed, it was noted that seizures were observed more oFSen in boys (58.3%) than in girls (41.7%).

he analysis of perinatal pathology showed that antenatal disorders were detected in 56.7% of cases and were oFSen manifested by gestosis (43.3% of children), while in the group of children with afebrile seizures, chronic fetoplacental insufficiency was detected in 5% of patients. Disturbances in the intranatal period were observed in 30% of the children we examined and were mainly associated with poor reproductive performance.

The cause of seizures in most cases was an infectious disease (88.3%), and the body temperature during a seizure was more than 38.0 oC in most cases (80% of all examined children). In this case, the risk of developing FS was high in children who were frequently sick.

In the group of patients with FS, a genetic predisposition to febrile seizures was observed in 30% of children, while in the group of patients with afebrile seizures, it was 10%. In the group of patients with FS, a genetic predisposition to afebrile seizures was found in 25% of children, while in the group of patients with afebrile seizures, it was 40%.

In the group of patients with FS, attacks appeared mainly before the age of 3 years (62.5% of children), in the group of patients with afebrile seizures, it was 80% of cases. In the FS group, seizures became generalized in 90% of patients, while in the AFS group, seizures became generalized in 60% of patients and focal in 40% of patients with secondary generalization.

When examining the neurological status, 65% of children with FS revealed pathology manifested by autonomic dysfunction, reflex field disorders, cerebral and discoordinating disorders. At this time, in the group of patients with AFS, neurostatus disorders occurred in 80% of children. In addition to the above disorders, hyperkinesis (30% of children) and pathological reflexes of children (15%) were observed in children with AFS. Delay in speech and psycho-speech development was observed most oFSen in children with AFS (80% of children), while in the group of patients with FS it was found in only 30% of children.

When the EEG was evaluated, changes in the general character of the brain in the form of a violation of the formation of age-related bioelectric activity at the bioelectric pace were observed in most children. Traces of bioelectrical activity in the brain were noted in 37.5% of examined children with FS and in 45% of children with AFS. In the group of patients with FS, alpha-rhythm instability was observed in 52.5% of children, and in the group of patients with afebrile seizures in 70% of cases. In the group of patients with FS, hypersynchronization was observed in 5% of children, while in the group of children with AFS, it was noted in only half of the examined children.

Brain MRI changes were observed in 7.5% of patients with FS, and in 25% of patients with AFS.

Chapter 3 Discussion

According to the literature [98,109], the most important factors in the development of FS include hyperthermia itself, the age of the patient, genetic predisposition, and perinatal pathology of the nervous system.

Our study found that among patients with FS, more children were 2-3 years old, which confirms the data reported in the literature [109,160,161,145], according to which FS occurs between the ages of 6 months and 5 years (with the peak of the disease occurring more oFSen at 1.5-2 years).). If we focus on the influence of gender in the development of FS, according to the results of a study [141], boys (around 60%) are more prone to the occurrence of FS.

A large number of researchers support the opinion that genetic predisposition is very important in the development of FS. The risk of developing FS increases if the parents also suffered from them [92,109,115,116,140,142], so, for example, if one of the parents has febrile seizures, then the risk of developing FS is 20%, if both parents have it - increases by 50% [130]. Among the types of genetic predisposition, autosomal-recessive, autosomal-dominant with partial penetrance, and the possibility of polygons are noted [125]. There are also data on the effect of a defect in the 2q23-24 gene on the development of

FS. Our work also shows the importance of the genetic factor in the development of febrile seizures, in 30% of children, the genetic predisposition is aggravated by the first family of relatives, and in 26.7% of children, it is aggravated by the first and second family.

Another important risk factor for the development of febrile seizures is the presence of perinatal pathology in the child [115,177,178,181]. L.O. According to Badalyan and co-authors (1988), more than 22% of children with FS have pathologies during pregnancy and delivery. If we talk about the pathologies of pregnancy, half of the children's mothers were diagnosed with fetal pathology of chronic hypoxia during pregnancy. Obstetrical pathologies are also important, so, for example, 21% of patients have prolonged labor, and 7.5% and 4.3% of children have asphyxia and umbilical cord wrapping. Separately, independently, risk factors are rare, their combination is usually observed. Thus, for example, according to some researchers [56,112], the combination of perinatal and genetic risk factors is the basis of the theory of "congenital disorders of the maturation process", which is due to brain immaturity, changes in bioelectric activity, inhibition and excitation processes occur, which, in turn, causes various paroxysmal conditions.

The presence of hyperthermia, as well as its level, is an important factor in the development of febrile seizures. In 75%

of patients, seizures develop when the body temperature rises to 39 °C, and in a quarter - at the level of 40 °C [4,142]. In our study, more than 55% of children had a body temperature of 38.5 oC during a seizure. Another important factor is the time period during which the temperature rises, in our study, a rapid increase in hyperthermia was found in half of all patients.

Concomitant diseases also affect the development of FS, for example, according to the literature [106,132,134,144,171] FS develops more ofSen against the background of acute respiratory and intestinal infections. At the same time, the risk of developing FS increases in children with frequent disease [180]. This was also noted in the data we received, so that, for example, almost 87% of children had FS on the background of ARVI, and 72% of children were found to have a high incidence of the disease.

Evaluation of the prognostic value of neurophysiological indicators has its own characteristics. In the period between attacks, most indicators can be normal. For example, EEG may correspond to the parameters of a healthy person in the period between attacks, and changes such as sharp waves and wave additions may occur in pathological conditions. According to Mukhin K. Yu and co-authors (2008), in the period between attacks, in patients with atypical febrile seizures, there is a continuous reciprocal slowing in more temporal networks. In our study, 76.7% of children had EEG periods between attacks consistent with those of healthy people, 20% of children had imperceptibly slowed down activity in the background, and 3% of children had paroxysms, in which epileptiform activity was not observed.

Risk factors for the development of repeated febrile attacks have been studied by many scientists [96,104,136,150,163,171,172]. According to many researchers, the most important and constant risk factor for the development of recurrent febrile attacks is age, namely the age at which the first case occurred [95,96,97,114,138,150,154,175].

Usually, the first episode of FS occurs at the age of 1.5 years, and in 90% of children, the onset of an attack corresponds to the age of 3 years, whereas attacks appear very rarely in children older than 5 years [98,104,107,109], that is, with age, the risk of recurrent attacks decreases [104,127,149], therefore, the younger the first episode, the greater the risk of recurrence [119]. In 50% of patients, relapse occurs in the first six months aFSer the onset, in 75% of children - within 2 years [97,104,107,109,149,150]. In our study, the onset of seizures occurred in most cases at 2 years of age and decreased with age, with recurrent attacks occurring within about 1 year.

Although boys suffer more from FS, this has not been confirmed in the literature as a risk factor for recurrent febrile seizures [104,149,150,171], which was also confirmed by our study.

Heredity also affects the risk of recurrence of febrile seizures, especially if FS is observed in first-degree relatives [116,127,154,163,172], which was partially confirmed in our study. For example, in patients whose febrile attacks occurred in two or more episodes, heredity was reliably aggravated in many cases.

In the literature, there is little information on the influence of perinatal pathology of the nervous system on the risk of recurrent febrile attacks [104,131], and despite the fact that the relationship between them was rarely determined in these studies, in our study, a statistically reliable correlation was found between pregnancy pathology and recurrent febrile attacks.

Regarding the influence of comorbidities on the risk of FS recurrence, we did not find a statistically significant correlation, but children with multiple diseases, mainly 3 or more cases of FS, were determined, which was also confirmed by some authors [171,176].

Summarizing the above, the data obtained from our research work do not differ from the results of other researchers, and the main risk factors for the onset of febrile seizures are genetic predisposition, perinatal pathology of the nervous system, and the risk factors of repeated FS are perinatal pathology, genetic predisposition, and the presence of infectious diseases. it can be said that it confirms the calculation.

Many researchers note that the presence of febrile seizures in the family history increases the risk of recurrent FS by 1.5-2 times, in which the severity of epilepsy is not less important [107,109,172].

As for the pathology of pregnancy, the analysis of the data provided in the literature did not show any relationship with the risk of developing recurrent FS. In our study, the pathology of pregnancy (chronic hypoxia of the fetus and the combination of chronic hypoxia with acute asphyxia) was found to be statistically reliable with the recurrence of febrile seizures.

CHAPTER 4.

RESULTS OF FEBRILE SEIZURES AND THEIR CLINICAL-NEUROLOGICAL AND NEUROPHYSIOLOGY DESCRIPTION. PREDICTIVE RISK FACTORS FOR THE TRANSFORMATION OF FEBRILE SEIZURES TO AFEBRILE SEIZURES.

4.1. Etiological, clinical-neurological and neurophysiological characteristics of the outcome of febrile seizures.

60 children aged 6 to 12 years (average age 11.6±2.35) with a history of febrile seizures were examined by a neurologist. Clinical, electroencephalographic, and neuroradiological examinations were conducted in ambulatory conditions. This group of patients was divided into subgroups according to the nature of febrile seizures: subgroup 1 - 30 children (13 girls and 17 boys) aged 8 to 15 years (mean age 1.11±2.44) with FS epilepsy. ; Subgroup 2 – 30 (10 girls and 20 boys) children with FS from 8 to 15 years (mean age 12.07±2.18).

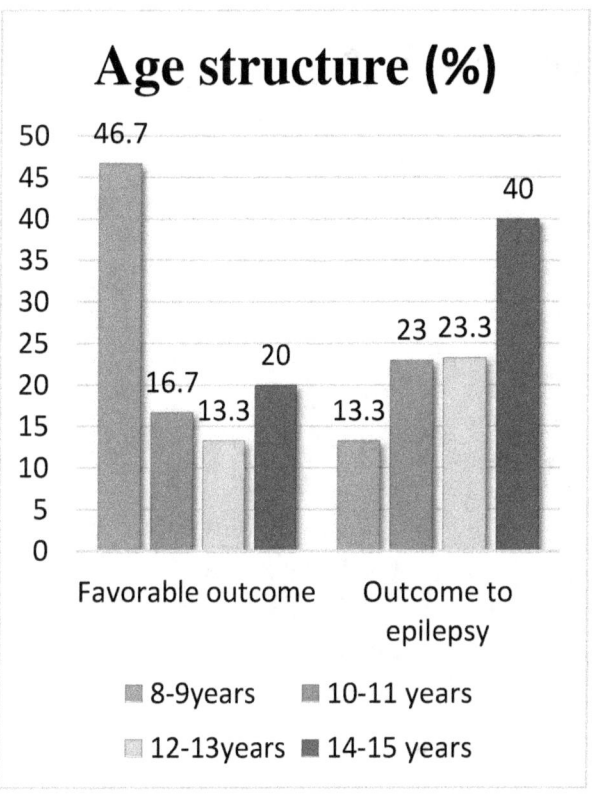

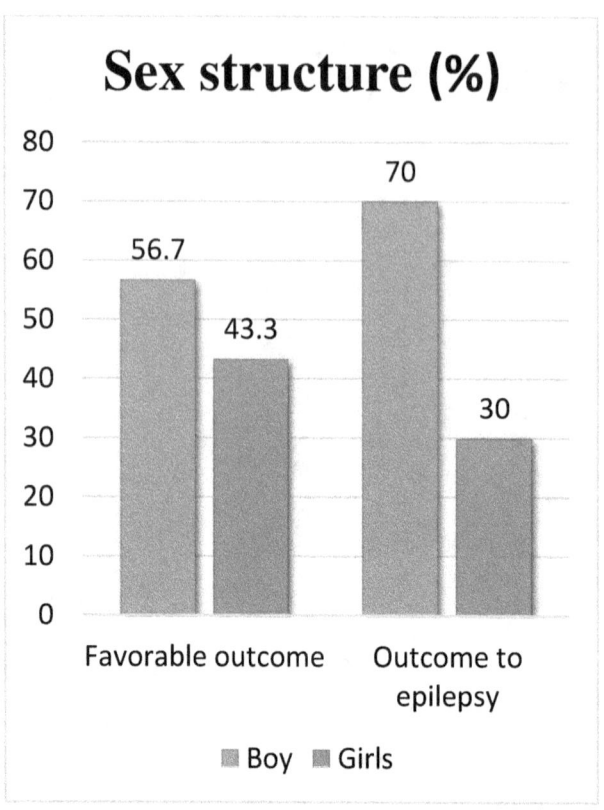

Figure 4.1 Age and gender indicators of children with FS in the anamnesis.

Among the total examined patients, boys constituted a reliable majority (63.3%), while in the comparison group boys and girls were 70% and 30%, respectively, the difference was less pronounced in the main group (56.7% boys and 43.3% girls).

In the main group of children, more symptomatic forms of epilepsy were found (83.3% of the examined children). Among them, the shape of the temple prevailed - 46.7%, followed by the shape of the forehead, which was observed in 26.7% of children, and the least defined shape was the shape of the back of the neck - 10% of children. In the temporal department, automotor seizures and temporal pseudoabsences were observed in almost half of the patients with a focal form of epilepsy, and in the rest of the patients, the seizures had a temporal-general character.

The general form of epilepsy was less common, 16.7% of children in the main group. 10% of children were diagnosed with childhood absence epilepsy, and less oFSen, 6.7% of children were diagnosed with juvenile form of absence epilepsy.

In one of our patients, the onset of epilepsy began with frequent atypical febrile seizures, which were focal in nature and did not bother him aFSer 5 years, he went into remission. But aFSer some time, the patient developed afebrile seizures, which gradually progressed to temporal epilepsy. It was found that the factor that led to the development of epilepsy was hippocampal sclerosis.

4.2. Risk factors influencing the transition of febrile seizures to epilepsy.

In order to determine the risk factors leading to febrile seizures, as well as to evaluate their prognostic value, we studied the genetic predisposition of patients, peculiarities of perinatal anamnesis, and clinical-neurological characteristics of patients.

Genetic factors play an important role in the development of febrile seizures and epilepsy. We determined the frequency of febrile seizures and epilepsy among relatives of children with febrile seizures who had a positive outcome and changed to epilepsy.

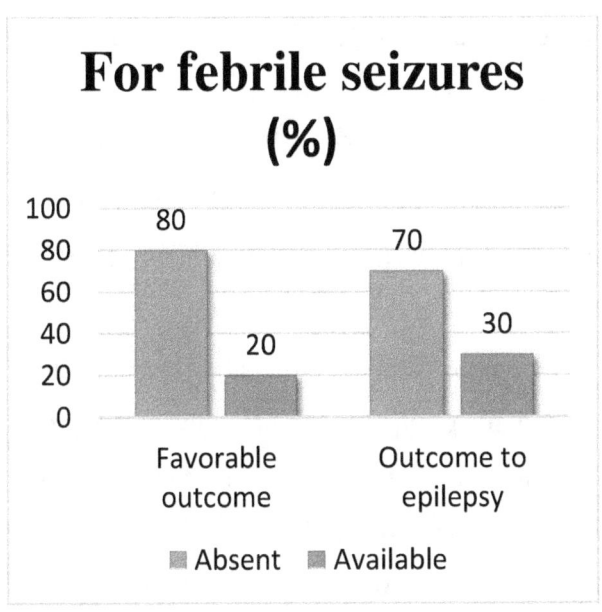
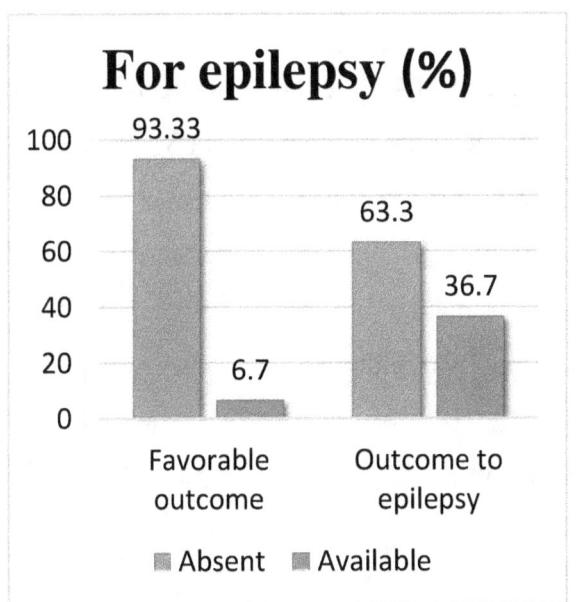

Figure 4.2 Frequency of febrile seizures and epilepsy among relatives of children with febrile seizures.

Hereditary aggravation of febrile seizures was found more oFSen in the main group (30%), while in the comparison group this indicator was equal to 20%. As for consanguinity, in both groups, the condition of genetic burden was mainly observed in first-degree relatives (20% in the main and 13.3% in the comparison group).

Hereditary complications of afebrile seizures predominated in the main group (36.7%), while in the group with a positive outcome, this figure was less than 30% and equaled only 6.7%. According to the degree of consanguinity, the genetic burden in this case was also more pronounced in first-degree relatives.

Factors that increase the likelihood of recurrence of febrile seizures include the clinical course of FS, as well as perinatal pathology, which can affect its subsequent changes.

We can directly observe the weakness of the reproductive function, premature births and cesarean delivery we studied the course of childbirth and antenatal period (presence of gestosis, risk of miscarriage and chronic fetoplacental insufficiency).

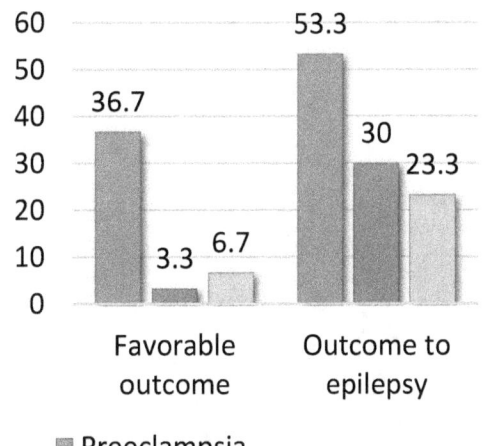

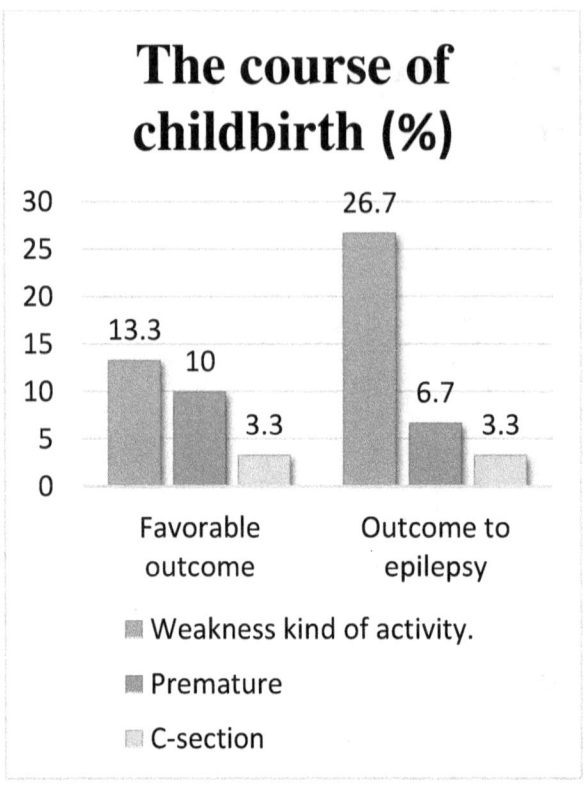

Figure 4.3 Factors that increase the likelihood of febrile seizures.

Disturbances in the antenatal period were observed in patients with epilepsy - 70%, in which more gestosis was detected in mothers (53.3%), and the risk of miscarriage was noted in 30% of mothers. It should be mentioned that chronic fetoplacental insufficiency was found in 23.3% of cases in the main group.

In patients of the comparison group, antenatal disorders were determined in 46.7% of cases, the risk of gestosis in mothers was determined in 36.7% of cases, and the risk of termination of pregnancy was determined in 6.7% of cases. Chronic fetoplacental insufficiency was detected in the mother of one patient (3.3% of cases).

When it comes to childbirth, in this case, 68.3% of the studied patients gave birth physiologically, on time. Weakness in reproductive performance was common, but no significant differences were found between groups, in 26.7% of cases in the main group, and 2 times less in the comparison group.

We analyzed the description of the debut of febrile seizures in children.

Table 4.2

Analysis of the description of the debut of febrile seizures in children.

	Core Group FSE		Comparison group FBI	
	N= 30	%	N= 30	%
Debut				
6 months. - 1 year old	11	36,7	10	33,3
1-3 years old	14	46,7	17	56,7
3-5 years old	5	16,7	3	10
The nature of the attack				
General	4	13,3	24	80
Fok. com. in common	23	76,7	5	16,7

with				
Focal	3	10	1	3,3
Number of seizures				
1-2 times	13	43,3	27	90
3–4 times	12	40	3	10
More than 4 times	5	16,7	0	0

In 51.7% of the children we examined, the onset of febrile seizures coincided with the age of 1-3 years, in 35%, febrile seizures began at one year of age, and in only 13.3% of children, FS began aFSer the age of 3 years. We did not observe a difference between the main group and the comparison group. According to the nature of the attacks, it can be said that there was a difference between the groups. In the main group, generalized seizures with a focal component prevailed (76.7%), while only generalized and focal seizures were detected in approximately equal amounts (13.3% and 10%, respectively). In the comparison group, on the contrary, generalized seizures prevailed (80% of children), generalized and focal seizures with a focal component were equal to 16.7% and 3.3%, respectively.

It was noted that in the comparison group, attacks occurred only 1-2 times in 90% of cases and were not observed more than 4 times, while in children of the main group, attacks were repeated 3-4 times in 40% of cases, and attacks were repeated more than 4 times in 16.7% of children.

When studying the neurological status, disorders in the neurological status were found in 61.7% of the examined patients. Disturbances in neurostatus were found more oFSen in the main group (96.7%), in the comparison group, focal symptoms were more oFSen found, in more than 26% of patients.

Table 4.3

Impairments in neurologic status when neurologic status was studied.

	Core Group FSE		Comparison group FS	
	N= 30	%	N= 30	%
Neurostatus				
Without changes	1	3,3	22	73,3
With no changes	29	96,7	8	26,7
Eye movement disorders	4	13,3	1	3,3
Ptosis	2	6,7	0	0
Let's complain	4	13,3	1	3,3
Nystagmus	4	13,3	1	3,3
Facial asymmetry	11	36,7	4	13,3
Smoothing of the nasolabial	12	40	5	16,7

fold				
Bulbar disorders	1	3,3	0	0
Dysarthria	8	26,7	1	3,3
Hyperkinesis	9	30	1	3,3
Violation of coordination of movements	5	16,7	1	3,3
Increased reflexes	20	66,7	7	23,3
Pathological reflexes	5	16,7	0	0
Vegetative dysfunction	21	70	11	36,7
Eye movement disorders	4	13,3	1	3,3

In the comparison group, when evaluating the neurological status, symptoms in the form of more widespread small foci, autonomic disorders were revealed, in 11 (36.7%) children, they were manifested in the form of profuse sweating and changes in the color of skin coverings. Increased tendon reflexes were observed in 7 (23.3%) children. Brain disorders in the form of flattening of the nasolabial fold and facial asymmetry were found in 13.3% of the examined children. Delay in speech and psycho-speech development was observed in 63.3% of children.

Neurostatus disorders were found more in children of the main group. As in the above group, children had the most autonomic dysfunction and reflex field disorders (70% and

66.7%, respectively), but in this group, the delay in speech and psycho-speech development came to the fore, it was noted in 86.7% of children. . Also, facial nerve pathologies in the form of facial asymmetry (36.7% of children) and smoothing of the nasolabial fold (40% of those examined), as well as squint (13%), nystagmus (13%) and ptosis (6.7%) were observed in this group of children. eye movement disorders and dysarthria (26.7%) were accompanied by hyperkinesis (30% of examined children) and pathological reflexes (16.7%), coordination disorders were noted in 15% of children.

The analysis of the results of electroencephalography showed that changes in the bioelectric activity of the brain were reliably more common in children in the main group (R<0.001) than in paients in the comparison group (10%).

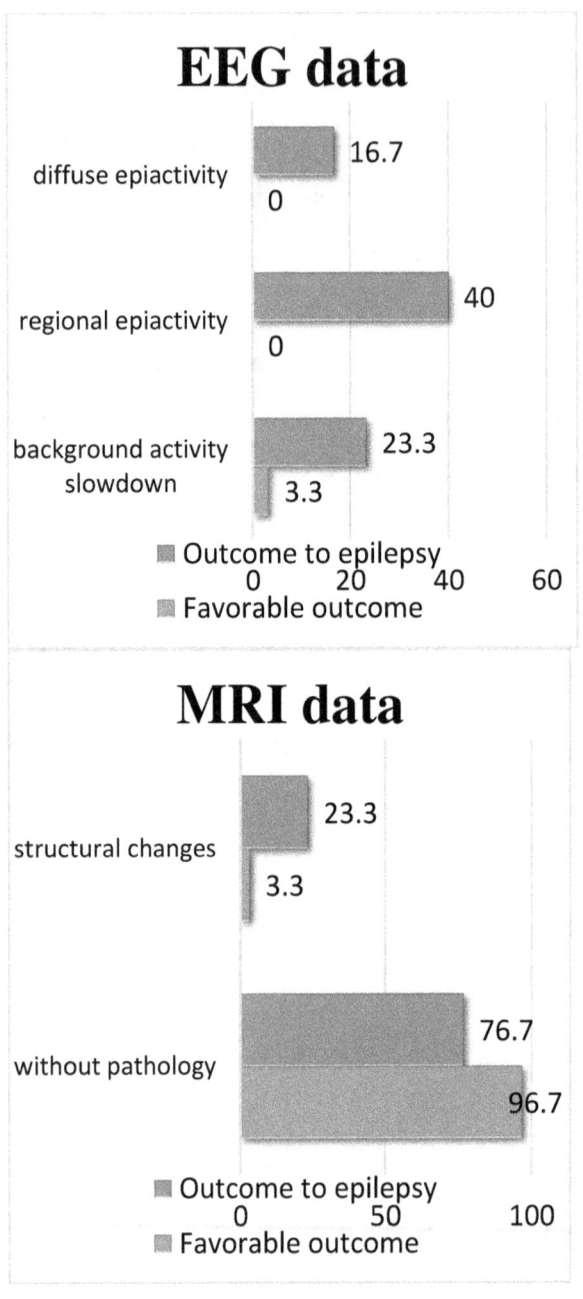

Figure 4.4 Neurophysiological investigations

In the electroencephalogram of patients in the main group, 23.3% of children showed disturbances in the form of background activity and 53.3% of children showed a slowing down of epileptic activity. On the other hand, epiactivity was diffuse in 16.7% of children, but was observed more regionally - 40% of children.

According to the results of magnetic resonance imaging, structural changes in the brain were statistically reliably detected in children of the main group (23.3%), while in the comparison group only one child (3.3%) had focal pathology (R<0.01). In the remaining cases, no changes were noted in the MRI results of the examined patients.

4.3. Prognosis of the development of epilepsy

In the previous chapters, we distinguished the indicators in which statistically significant differences were found in the examined groups. They included the presence of epilepsy in the family, the presence of a focal component in seizures, perinatal pathology, focal symptomatology: as well as pathological changes in neurophysiological research methods. We used a special method of multiple logistic regression to evaluate the prognostic significance of the above factors in the risk of febrile seizure transition to epilepsy.

For a more detailed assessment, a two-stage calculation was performed. Initially, we evaluated the two most common factors, genetic predisposition and focal symptomatology.

The observed relationship is described by the following model: 2 =21.25; df=2; (R<0.0001), the value of the constant: -2.5302. The heritability regression coefficient was 2.61 ± 0.711 with 95% II: 13.29 (3.35–53.21). The resulting model was statistically significant (r = 0.0003). The coefficient of regression of focal symptoms with 95% II was 1.19 ± 0.489: 3.34 (1.31–8.81). The resulting model was statistically significant (r = 0.0129). The area under the ROS-curve was 0.748 ± 0.0600 with 95% II: 0.673–0.813. The resulting model was statistically significant (r = 0.004).

It can be seen that although the factor we studied was reliably statistically significant, but the predictive character of the created model was low: that is, despite the high specificity of our model (96.8%), the sensitivity was very low (30.1%), this model is large, 3 ga 1 is likely to indicate in which patients FS will later have a positive outcome, in which children FS will progress to epilepsy.

In order to increase the effectiveness of the model, at the next stage, we added additional statistically significant indicators of clinical-technical studies. Due to the large number of choices and indicators, we used a stepwise exclusion method in constructing a logistic regression to exclude insignificant and mathematically small indicators and leave the most important factors for us. As a result, we distinguished 2 models: one model had the greatest diagnostic efficiency, and the other model had the minimum number of factors, with an insignificant loss of quality.

The observed relationship is described by the following model: $2 = 77.38$; $df=3$; ($R<0.0001$), the value of the constant: -3.3608. Neurostatus disorders, slow-wave sleep pathology on EEG were excluded from the model. The coefficient of heritability regression was 2.51 ± 0.977 with 95% CI: 12.02 (1.77–82.38). The resulting model was statistically significant ($r=0.0109$). The coefficient of epileptiform activity in EEG was 3.73 ± 1.661 with 95% II: 43.93 (1.69–1094.1). The resulting model was statistically significant ($r=0.0228$). The coefficient of alertness disturbance in EEG was 2.09 ± 1.306 with 95% II: (0.642–107.31), but the obtained model was not statistically significant ($r=0.1057$). The area under the ROS-curve was 0.911 ± 0.0438 with 95% II: 0.849–0.951. The resulting model was statistically significant ($r<0.01$). The sensitivity and specificity of the model were 71.2% and 98.1%, respectively. Diagnostic efficiency was 85.1% in 93.9% correctly classified.

The information we obtained allows us to predict the transition of FS to epilepsy based on the genetic burden of epilepsy and the presence of changes in the electroencephalogram. In doing so, these models revealed that the most valuable and reliable prognostic factor in EEG is the presence of epileptiform activity.

The observed relationship is described by the following model: $\chi^2 = 76.12$; df=2; (R<0.0001), the value of the constant: -3.2811. Neurostatus disorders, EEG alertness and slow wave sleep pathology were excluded from the model. The heritability regression coefficient was 3.00 ± 0.877 at 95% II: 19.96 (3.62–112.41). The obtained model was statistically significant (r=0.0006. The coefficient of epileptiform activity in EEG was 5.81 ± 1.127 at 95% II: 323.6 (34.9–2963.3). The obtained model was statistically significant (r<0.0001). The area under the ROS-curve was 0.891 ± 0.0489 at 95% II: 0.827–0.926. The resulting model was statistically significant (r<0.01). The sensitivity and specificity of the model, respectively 67.1% and 99.3%, respectively.Diagnostic efficiency was 83.4%, with the number of correctly classified - 93.3%.

So, for example, for the best model, if the patient has information about the presence of epilepsy in his relatives only in the anamnesis, i.e. hereditary weight, then the calculation gives the probability of placing the patient in the risk group equal to 0.429, that is, there is no risk. In this case, even if there is no genetic predisposition to epilepsy, in the presence of epiactivity in the patient's EEG, the probability of transition of FS to epilepsy is very high and the risk is estimated at 0.913. If both factors are present, the probability of FS progressing to epilepsy is estimated at 0.997.

Chapter 4 Discussion

As a result of examining patients with a history of febrile seizures, we found that the main group had more young children, and the comparison group consisted of older children. The average age in the examined groups was 11.1±2.44 and 12.07±2.18, respectively.

Boys predominated among those examined in both groups, but the difference in the main group was insignificant.

In the main group, more symptomatic forms of epilepsy were found in children (83.3% of examined children). Among them, the shape of the temple prevailed - 46.7% were children.

The genetic burden of febrile seizures was higher in the main group (30%), compared to 20% in the comparison group. Hereditary burden of afebrile seizures was reliably dominant in the main group (36.7%), while in the group with a positive outcome, this indicator was 30% less, equal to 6.7%.

Disturbances during pregnancy were most oFSen noted in patients with epilepsy - 70%, in which gestosis predominated in mothers (53.3%), and XFPN was found in 23.3% of mothers in the main group. Among patients of the comparison group, disorders also prevailed in the antenatal period (46.7%), the leading factor was gestosis (36.7% of children). The intranatal period was disturbed in 31.7% of mothers, which was manifested by weakness in labor activity in the main group, but the difference between the groups was not detected.

As for the timing of childbirth, in this case, it was determined that in 68.3% of the patients we examined, childbirth occurred physiologically and on time. Frailty in labor was the most common, but no significant difference between groups was observed, it was found in 26.7% of mothers in the main group, and 2 times less in the comparison group.

In 51.7% of the children we examined, the onset of febrile seizures corresponded to the age of 1-3 years. We found no difference between the main group and the comparison group. As for the nature of seizures, general seizures with a focal component prevailed in the main group (76.7% of patients), while in the comparison group, on the contrary, generalized seizures were more common (80% of children).

Neurological status disorders were found in 61.7% of examined children. Disturbances in neurostatus were found more oFSen in the main group (96.7%) and they were expressed at a severe level, while in the comparison group focal symptoms were slightly more identified and observed in more than 26% of patients.

Disturbances in the rate of bioelectrical activity of the brain were more reliably detected in children of the main group (80%) than in the comparison group (10%). A similar trend was observed in neuroimaging, where structural changes in the brain were detected more reliably in children in the main group

(23.3%), compared to 3.3% of children in the comparison group.

If we take information from the old literature about febrile seizures, as well as their ending, then we can find different, sometimes contradictory opinions. Such a wide range of opinions can be attributed primarily to the fact that there is no single definition of febrile seizures, as well as different approaches to research, patient selection, and study duration.

Current data suggest that febrile seizures are a condition associated with positive quality, age, and heredity [120,157]. However, in up to 30% of cases, febrile seizures are considered the debut variant of some epilepsy syndromes [54,103]. Shorvon et al., (2013), according to some studies[147,167], the probability of febrile seizures progressing to epilepsy ranges from 2% to 7%, depending on the nature of the febrile seizures. According to [46,103], typical forms of febrile seizures change in most cases to either positive-quality focal epilepsy or, in 10-20% of cases, to idiopathic generalized epilepsy [103, 108], in which atypical forms of febrile seizures are symptomatic temporal epilepsy, Dravé syndrome [54], it is also detected at the beginning of myoclonic epilepsy. Other data [158] show that 15–30% of patients with symptomatic temporal lobe epilepsy have atypical forms of febrile seizures.

In a number of cases, the authors [55,110] note the variant status of febrile seizures. In our study, focal forms of epileptic seizures were mainly manifested by atypical febrile seizures (76.7% - common with a focal component, 10% - focal). In 2 patients, febrile seizures progressed to juvenile absence epilepsy, in 2 more cases to childhood epilepsy.

Analyzing the data in the literature, it was found that the main risk factors for the transition of FS to epilepsy are genetic predisposition, premorbid background, as well as the presence of atypical febrile seizures in the anamnesis [61,118,153,160,162]. is an atypical character of variable seizures. Data from Pavlidou E. et al., (2013) show that only 2% of typical forms of febrile seizures progress to epilepsy, while 4-6% of patients with atypical seizures have a high risk of transition to epilepsy, and 5% in febrile status. According to other sources [111], the risk of progression to epilepsy in complex FSs is 16%–20%. Typical febrile seizures have a 4% chance of becoming afebrile, while atypical febrile seizures have a 92% chance [4].

Based on the data obtained from studies [70,118,133,139,182], it can be said with confidence that genetic weight, complex type of attack, and psycho-neurological disorders are significant factors that increase the risk of febrile seizures becoming afebrile.

According to the results of our work, it can be noted that the genetic factor, focal type of attacks, focal symptoms in neurostatus are predictors of developing epilepsy in patients with FS. In this case, the presence of epilepsy in the family history was more reliably determined in patients with epilepsy (R<0.001), in 76.7% of examined patients with epilepsy, FS had a common character with a focal component, and in 10% - focal character of seizures was determined. In neurostatus, focal symptoms were observed in 53.3% of children, and focal disorders were noted in only 26.7% of patients with a positive result of FS.

EEG cannot be definitively accepted as a risk factor for the transition of febrile seizures to epilepsy, taking into account the different characteristics of the age of patients, as well as the time of onset of seizures [164]. An analysis of some literature data [124,140] showed that no correlation was found between focal phenomena on EEG and the development of afebrile seizures (epilepsy), but some authors [143] reported that the presence of paroxysmal focal phenomena on EEG was more common in patients with FS epilepsy than in patients with a positive outcome. They reported that they were identified 5 times. Sofijanov et al. (1992) found in their study that children with atypical febrile seizures lasting at least 15 minutes had more paroxysmal phenomena on EEG.

Epileptiform paroxysms of focal deceleration type [148] can be observed in febrile status. Other literature data also confirmed that epileptic paroxysms were detected in the EEG of patients with FS, which can be evaluated as a risk factor for the transition of FS to epilepsy [16,33,73,78,126,129,135,183].

On the other hand, the data of Doose H. et al., (2000) emphasize that the presence of epileptiform paroxysms in the electroencephalography of patients under 5 years of age testifies to a predisposition to epilepsy, that is, not as a prognostic factor for the transition of FS to AFS, but to a congenital disorder in the formation of the brain.

In our study, 76.7% of children who ended up with epilepsy had pathology detected in the EEG, while in the group of patients with a positive outcome, this indicator was equal to 3.3%.

Some literature data indicate the influence of structural changes in the brain on the transition of febrile seizures to epilepsy [121,123,151]. Studies on mesial temporal sclerosis are very widespread, for example, some authors [99,109,145] found a difference between the formation of MVS against the background of febrile seizures, other researchers note that febrile seizures occur in only 1-2% of patients with MVS, and H. Holthausen (1997) in his reported that febrile seizures occurred in 18-79% of patients with MVS in their study, and gave generally different data. The problem with these studies is their low follow-up, since at least 5-10 years are required for FS to progress to epilepsy.

Our study showed that 23.3% of children with epilepsy had pathological changes on MRI, while in the comparison group, changes were observed in only 3.3% of children.

Summarizing the above, it is worth noting that genetic predisposition, the presence of focal disturbances in the neurostatus, the presence of a focal component in an attack can be considered as an open prognostic factor of the risk of transitioning to an afebrile form of FS, while the pathological changes identified in neurophysiological research methods are risk factors that increase this possibility.

CHAPTER 5.
COMPARATIVE COMPREHENSIVE NEUROPSYCHOLOGICAL EXAMINATION DATA IN PATIENTS WITH A HISTORY OF FEBRILE AND AFEBRIL SEIZURES AND FEBRILE SEIZURES.

5.1. Data from a comprehensive neuropsychological examination of patients with a positive qualitative outcome of febrile seizures.

We used several methods to assess neuropsychological development, taking into account the different age groups of the children we examined. To examine children under 5 years of age, we used the Denver psychomotor development test, and to study children with a history of FS, we used the Wechsler intelligence test (WISC – Wechsler Intelligence Scale for Children) and L.I. Wassermana, E.D. Khomskoy, L.S. Tsvetkovoy, A.B. Partially modified using the methods of Semenovich, traditional A.R. We used a battery of Lurie tests.

As for individual indicators of the Denver test, we found a difference between the groups. Among the patients, more fine motor disorders (61.7%) were observed, which was found in the group with more afebrile seizures (75% of children), while in the TFS and ATFS group, it was 50% and 60% of children, respectively.

Next in prevalence were speech disorders observed in 55% of the examined children, which were the least detected in the group of children with TFS (45%), slightly more in the group of children with ATFS (55%) and the most detected in the group of children with AFS - 65 % children.

Gross motor impairment was observed in half of the children we examined. In this case, it was also found more oFSen in the group of afebrile seizures (65% of children), while in the group of children with typical seizures, this indicator was almost 2 times lower, equal to 35%, and in the group of ATFS - 50%.

Individual-social disorders were observed in the least cases. In the group with simple febrile seizures, these disorders were observed in 30% of children with TFS, while in the group of patients with ATFS they were observed 1.5 times more, and in the group of patients with afebrile seizures 2 times.

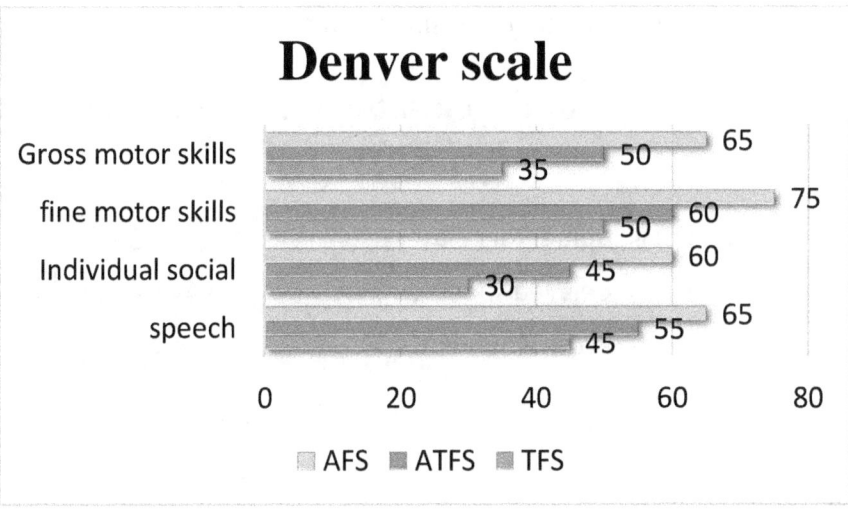

Figure 5.1 Denver Developmental Test (DDST) patient scores

Combining the data of the Denver scale, we distinguished 3 types of psychomotor development: normative, speech development and delay of fine motor skills, general delay of psychomotor development.

Analysis of Denver Scale data showed that in the group with typical febrile seizures, 8 (40%) patients had age-matched psychomotor development on all 4 measures, 7 (35%) patients had speech development and fine motor delay, 5 (25%) and a general developmental delay was noted in the child.

In the group with atypical febrile seizures, up to 30% of patients had a delay in normal development and general development, while 40% of patients had a delay in speech development and fine motor skills in the hands.

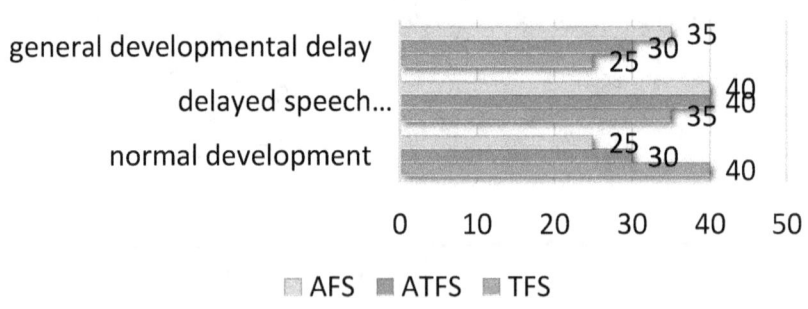

5.2 The Denver Developmental Test (DDST) is a developmental type

The most pronounced changes were noted in the group with afebrile seizures, where 35% of children had a delay in general development, 40% of children had a delay in speech development and fine motor skills, and only 25% of patients were assessed as developmentally normal.

Later, we conducted a neuropsychological study in children with FS, and in the anamnesis we used the Wechsler intelligence test (WISC – Wechsler Intelligence Scale for Children) and A.R. We used Lurii's modified battery of tests.
When we evaluated the children according to the Wechsler scale, we found the following changes. Overall, children with FS transitioned to epilepsy scored lower than children with a positive outcome, as expected, and verbal intelligence scores were nonsignificantly higher than nonverbal intelligence scores.

In a study of nonverbal intelligence in patients with FS transitioning to epilepsy, children with FSE had the greatest problems with tests of coordination and attention, a scrambling test, and tests of putting parts together, as in verbal intelligence.

When verbal intelligence was studied in patients with epilepsy, small difficulties were observed in tests of vocabulary, where it was necessary to identify concepts and explain the meaning of words, and in tests of similarity, in which children had problems with identifying and distinguishing objects by some common features. Children performed the awareness and comprehension tests easily.

Then, based on the obtained scores, we determined the intelligence level of the examined children and obtained the following information.

Assessment of mental development according to the scale of Wechsler (WISC).

Indicators	FS	FSE
Medium and above medium	7 (23,3%)	5 (16,7%)
The lower limit of the norm	11 (36,7%)	7 (23,3%)
Border area	12 (40%)	11 (36,7%)
Mental retardation	0 (0%)	7 (23,3%)

In the group of FS epilepsy, in 7 patients, we established a diagnosis of mental retardation, while in the group with a positive outcome, no such changes were observed. In the group with a positive result, the results of the borderline area and the lower limit of the norm were found (40% and 36.7% of children), average and above-average intelligence was found in 23.3% of patients. In the group that changed to epilepsy, borderline intelligence was found in 36.7% of patients, while subnormal and average and above-average intelligence were observed in 23.3% and 16.7% of patients, respectively.

Then, A.R. We have conducted a comprehensive neuropsychological study of Lurie's modified complex tests.

Examination of motor functions in children with good-quality febrile seizures showed that 23.3% of children had mild impairments, so that, for example, the test using the piano, its reverse order, caused difficulties for the examinees, in particular, these children performed a sequence of movements. they made mistakes. Also, graphic tests in these children led to difficulties, namely, an increase in the time spent on performing tasks, a violation of the sequence of objects.

Kinesthetic praxis was impaired in 13.3% of patients, especially strongly expressed in these tests when the eyes were closed, in such cases it was difficult for the children to distinguish fingers or transfer certain positions from one hand to another and vice versa.

Another 23.3% of children were found to have impairments in hand-reciprocal coordination tests, mostly at the mild and moderate levels (13.3% and 10%, respectively). In this case, the children had difficulty controlling the given rhythm, as well as changing between different hands and rhythms.

One of the most common disorders in children with a positive outcome was spatial praxis disorder, which was found in more than half of the children (53.3%). In this case, disorders were either mild (33.3% of children) or moderate - 20.0% of children. Some tests, such as Benton and Denman, were clearly and correctly performed by our children. Almost all children made mistakes when performing the sensitization test aimed at reflecting spatial images. The Khod test resulted in errors in 43.3% of patients, and the open version in 40% of children, where 16.7% of children had difficulty performing this test with verbal commands. Another test in which 26.7% of children were impaired was the Ray-Asterits test, in which children experienced difficulties in the spatial arrangement of shapes, as well as in their internal elements or in misrepresenting the sizes and determining their compatibility with other object elements.

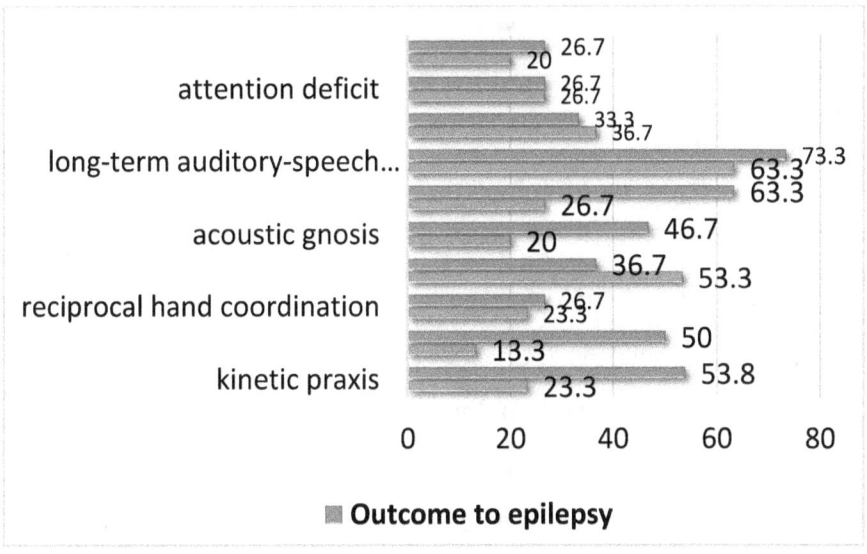

Figure 5.7 Neuropsychological changes (%) in children with febrile seizures ending in good-quality seizures

Analysis of visual-spatial gnosis revealed pathology in about 20% of patients. In this case, the children had disorders when trying to identify letters, numbers or objects that were hidden or painted off, but in general, when identifying objects or numbers and letters or reading and recognizing colors, no problems were found in the examined patients.

In the next place, our patients' correct performance of calculations was checked. Performing calculations while reading or writing, as well as seeing numbers in the same configuration and spatial understanding did not cause difficulties for the patients. But at the same time, in 20% of patients, difficulties were found when the tests were complicated. When serial and automated counting was checked, disorders were noted in 36.7% of children, of which 23.3% were mild and 13.3% were moderate.

Then we examined the function of acoustic reception in children (acoustic gnosis). First, we ran a test asking the children to identify familiar sounds, and all the children did perfectly. Then, in the tests of auditory-motor coordination, in 20% of children we found violations in the form of violations in repeating the proposed rhythm, and in 6.7% of children, violations were noted when the rhythm was complicated (for example, additional beats appeared).

The memory of our patients was also tested in many different ways. We examined general memory, auditory and speech (short-term and long-term), visual-object memory. All our patients successfully passed the general and visual-object memory tests. However, when auditory-speech memory was tested, many children had problems. In our long-term auditory speech memory test, we asked children to memorize a word by saying it, then asking them to say it an hour later, and we plotted a curve based on the response. Impairment of long-term auditory verbal memory was the most common impairment in the children we examined and accounted for 63.3%, 20% of children had impairments of moderate severity, and 43.3% had mild impairment. To test children's short-term auditory-speech memory, we asked them to remember words and phrases, specific sentences and sentences. Short-term auditory-verbal memory showed impairment in 26.7% of children (6.7% - moderate level and 20% mild level), this is especially the case with the addition of a special load in the form of counting down or reciting a small text or, for example, adding physical exercises. was expressed more when it was complicated.

The analysis of attention disorders using the Schulte table revealed disorders in the speed of attention switching, as well as attention span and performance speed in 26.7% of children. In addition, a test was conducted to study the ability to maintain attention for a certain period of time, which revealed a disorder in the form of a decrease in attention in 20% of patients, which was oFSen of moderate severity.

Children with FS progression to epilepsy had significantly more and more severe psychoneurological disorders. In total, disorders were detected in 26 (86.7%) children, and only 4 had a standard variant. The results of the examination showed that the most common disorders of motor functions were, for example, 53.3% of children had kinetic praxis disorders, while 30% of patients had the disorder was moderate, and 23.3% had a mild level, so that, for example, the test using the piano, its exact reverse order, or speeding up the pace of the test, caused difficulties for the test subjects, in particular, these children made mistakes when performing the sequence of actions. Another common test, fist-side-palm, caused less difficulty, but even then, item-switching disorders were observed, which were mainly associated with increasing the speed of the test or changing the tempo. Also in these children (40%) graphic tests caused difficulties, exactly 23.3% of patients spent time on tasks multiplication and disruption of the sequence of objects.

Kinesthetic praxis was impaired in half of the examined patients, which was especially pronounced when the eyes were closed in these tests. Children with mild impairment had difficulty separating fingers or moving certain positions from one hand to the other and vice versa.

Another 26.7% of children were found to have impairments in hand-reciprocal coordination testing, which were mostly mild and moderate (16.7% and 10%, respectively). In this condition, children had difficulty controlling a given rhythm, as well as switching between different hands and rhythms in the Ozeretsky test or in the reciprocal tapping test. We also examined oral praxis, which was found to be unimpaired in all patients.

One of the most common disorders in children with epilepsy was the disorder of spatial praxis, which was found in more than half of all children (60%). At the same time, disorders were either mild (26.7% of children) or of moderate severity - 33.3% of children.

Some tests, such as Denman and Benton, were performed satisfactorily by the examinees. All children made errors when performing the sensitization version of the test, which is a task of reflecting spatial images. Taylor's test showed problems in the rhythm of the tasks, the children incorrectly repeated different parts of the shapes, or incorrectly drew straight lines. The examined children had difficulty in spatial placement of shapes, as well as their internal elements, or wrongly choosing sizes and determining their compatibility with other elements of objects.

53.3% and 43.3% of patients performed the Khod test with errors, and 20% of children had difficulties with the speed of execution of the test, incorrect placement of limbs, etc., which was especially evident when performing this test with spoken commands, but it became easier to repeat aFSer the researcher.

Analysis of visual spatial gnosis revealed pathology in 26.7% of patients. In this case, children made errors when they tried to identify letters, numbers or objects that were hidden or painted over, but the patients we examined did not have problems with reading and finding colors.

In the analysis of object gnosis, as well as in color, letter gnosis, and reading, 23.3% of patients were found to have disorders.

Then, our patients were checked for correct arithmetic operations. Our patients performed successfully in many cases, such as performing arithmetic operations while reading or writing, seeing numbers in the same configuration, and spatial comprehension tests. In 30% of patients, difficulties were found when the tests were complicated. When serial and automated counting was checked, disorders were found in 43.3% of children, of which 23.3% were mild and 20% were moderate.

Then we examined the acoustic reception activity in children (acoustic gnosis). First, we conducted tests to assess the perception of non-speech sounds (sound images) and also assigned tasks in which we asked the children to identify familiar sounds, which all children succeeded in doing. Then, in tests of auditory-monitor coordination, we found impairments in 46.7% of children, in which 5 (16.7%) patients had mild impairments, 9 (30%) patients had moderate impairments. The main types of violations were performing at the suggested tempo, making additional beats, partial or complete violation of the given rhythm, in particular, errors in the text, as well as individual perseverations.

The memory of our patients was also tested in various ways. We examined general memory, auditory speech (short-term and long-term), visual object memory. Most of our patients successfully completed the tests when general and visual object memory were studied, only 4 (13.3%) patients had impairments. Mainly, the problems arose in the examination of auditory speech memory. In the long-term auditory speech memory test, we told children words, asked them to memorize the words, and asked them to say them an hour later, and thus constructed a curve based on this. Impairment of long-term auditory speech memory was the most common impairment in the children we examined and accounted for 73.3%, 43.3% of children had moderate impairment, and 30% of children had mild impairment. To test short-term auditory speech memory, we asked children to memorize words and phrases, special sentences and sentences. Examination of short-term auditory speech memory showed impairment in 63.3% of children (30% - moderate and 33.3% mild), especially when these tests were complicated by adding a special load in the form of counting backwards or reciting a small text or, for example, adding physical exercises. expressed a lot.

The analysis of attention disorders using the Schulte table showed disorders in 43.3% of children (in 26.7% of patients, the disorders had a moderate level of severity, and in 16.7% of children, the level of mild severity), which is mainly in the violation of the speed of attention, as well as the volume of attention and the speed of work. manifested in the violation. In addition, a test examining the ability to maintain attention over time was conducted, which revealed impairments in the form of attention deficit in 26.7% of patients, which were oFSen moderate.

Thus, the study of psycho-speech disorders in patients with a history of febrile seizures showed that when the disease progresses to afebrile paroxysms, there is a delay in mental and psycho-speech development. this requires the maximum early involvement of not only medication, but also cognitive correction methods.

DISCUSSION

Febrile seizures (seizures, FS) are the most common variant of paroxysmal conditions in pediatric practice today. These episodes of epileptic seizures occur in preschool children with hyperthermia and are not associated with neuroinfection. FS is a benign, age-related, genetically determined condition in which the brain becomes susceptible to epileptic seizures in response to high temperatures. In children of preschool age, FS is considered transient in most cases, but at the same time it can be part of separate epileptic syndromes [Pavlidou E, Panteliadis C.2013., Chung S.2014, Dolinina A.F., Gromova L.L., Mukhin K. Yu., 2015]. The prevalence of febrile seizures in children aged 6 months to 6 years is 2-5% [Ismailova N.B. 2013., Musabekova T.O., 2014, Olimov A.R., 7017.,].

In many cases, seizures are life-threatening. The death rate among patients with epilepsy is 2-3 times higher than the death rate in the population, therefore, the age of maturation of the brain and the occurrence of febrile seizures "is a determinant of the risk of recurrence, the younger the age at the onset of seizures, the higher the risk of recurrence" [Fallah. et al. , 2010., Guzeva V.I. 2012, Alexin A.N., Turovskaya N.G. 2013,].

It should be noted that recently there is evidence that a small proportion of children may develop neurological deficits aFSer FS, FS or epilepsy relapse, learning problems, movement disorders and behavioral changes, unspecialized sensory symptoms and memory failure [Manreza M.L., Gherpelli J.L., Machado-Haertel L.R., et al., Berg A.T., Shinnar S. 2010., Wasserman L.I. 2015., Zavadenko A.N. 2016], which requires prompt assistance to children with FS, timely correction of disorders [Sharipov A.M., Olimov A.R., Khakimov J.P. 2017].

The purpose of our research is to study psycho-speech development in febrile seizures, its clinical-neurological, paraclinical specific features, determining the correlation of indicators.

The study is based on the results of clinical-neurological and instrumental analyzes of 120 patients with various degrees of FS admitted for inpatient and outpatient treatment at the regional multidisciplinary medical center and private neurology clinics in Bukhara during 2016-2020.

In the first phase, 60 patients with febrile seizures between 6 months and 5 years of age (mean age 3.4±1.15) who met the study inclusion criteria were treated in the neurology department to study the clinical characteristics of febrile seizures, their recurrence and risk factors for afebrile transition. A group of children (35 boys and 25 girls) was separated. We divided this group of patients into 3 subgroups according to the nature of febrile seizures: subgroup 1 - with typical febrile seizures, 20 patients (6 girls and 14 boys) aged 6 months to 5 years (average age 3.0±1.17) children) child; Subgroup 2 - 20 children (8 girls and 12 boys) aged 6 months to 5 years (average age 3.2±1.06) with atypical febrile seizures; Subgroup 3 - 20 (8 girls and 12 boys) children aged 6 months to 5 years (average age 4±1.03) with afebrile seizures.

In the second stage, a study of 60 patients with a history of febrile seizures, under the observation of a neurologist, aged 8 to 15 years (mean age 11.6±2.35). Clinical, electroencephalographic, neuroradiological examinations were carried out in ambulatory conditions. We divided this group of patients into 2 subgroups according to the nature of febrile seizures: subgroup 1 – 30 children aged 8 to 15 years (mean age 1.11±2.44) who ended with FS epilepsy; In subgroup 2 - 30 children (10 girls and 20 boys) aged 8 to 15 years (mean age 12.07±2.18) with atypical febrile seizures.

A questionnaire was developed for registration. It contains data on perinatal history, genetic factors (presence of epilepsy, febrile seizures in relatives), causes of seizures (temperature, degree of temperature rise, background disease, frequency of diseases), information on the nature, frequency and duration of febrile seizures, neurological status and additional examination. results of methods (EEG, EEG-video-monitoring, CT, MRI) are included. Diagnosis of epilepsy in children was made according to the criteria recommended by the International Classification of Epilepsy and Epileptic Syndromes (1989).

When we studied children with febrile and afebrile seizures, it was found that FS was more oFSen observed in 2- and 3-year-old children (55%), while in the group of children with AFS, on the contrary, 4- and 5-year-old patients made up the majority - 70%. When gender differences were analyzed, it was noted that seizures were observed more oFSen in boys (58.3%) than in girls (41.7%). Our study found that among patients with FS, more children were 2-3 years old, which confirms the data reported in the literature [109,160,161,145], according to which FS occurs between the ages of 6 months and 5 years (with the peak of the disease occurring more oFSen at 1.5-2 years).). If we focus on the influence of gender in the development of FS, according to the results of a study [141], boys (around 60%) are more prone to the occurrence of FS.

Another important risk factor for the development of febrile seizures is the presence of perinatal pathology in the child [115,177,178,181]. L.O. According to Badalyan and co-authors (1988), more than 22% of children with FS have pathologies during pregnancy and delivery. If we talk about the pathologies of pregnancy, half of the children's mothers were diagnosed with fetal pathology of chronic hypoxia during pregnancy. Obstetrical pathologies are also important, so, for example, 21% of patients have prolonged labor, and 7.5% and 4.3% of children have asphyxia and umbilical cord wrapping. Separately, independently, risk factors are rare, their combination is usually observed. The analysis of perinatal pathology showed that antenatal disorders were detected in 56.7% of cases and were oFSen manifested by gestosis (43.3% of children), while in the group of children with afebrile seizures, chronic fetoplacental insufficiency was detected in 5% of patients. Disturbances in the intranatal period were observed in 30% of the children we examined and were mainly associated with poor reproductive performance.

The presence of hyperthermia, as well as its level, is an important factor in the development of febrile seizures. In 75% of patients, seizures develop when the body temperature rises to 39 °C, and in a quarter - at the level of 40 °C [4,142]. In our study, more than 55% of children had a body temperature of 38.5 oC during a seizure. Another important factor is the time period during which the temperature rises, in our study, a rapid increase in hyperthermia was found in half of all patients.

A large number of researchers support the opinion that genetic predisposition is very important in the development of FS. The risk of developing FS increases if the parents also suffered from them [92,109,115,116,140,142], so, for example, if one of the parents has febrile seizures, then the risk of developing FS is 20%, if both parents have it - increases by 50% [130]. In the group of patients with FS, a genetic predisposition to febrile seizures was observed in 30% of children, while in the group of patients with afebrile seizures, it was 10%. In the group of patients with FS, a genetic predisposition to afebrile seizures was found in 25% of children, while in the group of patients with afebrile seizures, it was 40%.

Usually, the first episode of FS occurs at the age of 1.5 years, and in 90% of children, the onset of an attack corresponds to the age of 3 years, whereas attacks appear very rarely in children older than 5 years [98,104,107,109], that is, with age, the risk of recurrent attacks decreases [104,127,149], therefore, the younger the first episode, the greater the risk of recurrence [119].

In the group of patients with FS, attacks appeared mainly before the age of 3 years (62.5% of children), in the group of patients with afebrile seizures, it was 80% of cases. In the FS group, seizures became generalized in 90% of patients, while in the AFS group, seizures became generalized in 60% of patients and focal in 40% of patients with secondary generalization.

When examining the neurological status, 65% of children with FS revealed pathology manifested by autonomic dysfunction, reflex field disorders, cerebral and discoordinating disorders. At this time, in the group of patients with AFS, neurostatus disorders occurred in 80% of children. In addition to the above disorders, hyperkinesis (30% of children) and pathological reflexes of children (15%) were observed in children with AFS. Delay in speech and psycho-speech development was observed most oFSen in children with AFS (80% of children), while in the group of patients with FS it was found in only 30% of children.

Evaluation of the prognostic value of neurophysiological indicators has its own characteristics. In the period between attacks, most indicators can be normal. For example, EEG may correspond to the parameters of a healthy person in the period between attacks, and changes such as sharp waves and wave additions may occur in pathological conditions. According to Mukhin K. Yu and co-authors (2008), in the period between attacks, in patients with atypical febrile seizures, there is a continuous reciprocal slowing in more temporal networks.

When the EEG was evaluated, changes in the general character of the brain in the form of a violation of the formation of age-related bioelectric activity at the bioelectric pace were observed in most children. Traces of bioelectrical activity in the brain were noted in 37.5% of examined children with FS and in 45% of children with AFS. In the group of patients with FS, alpha-rhythm instability was observed in 52.5% of children, and in the group of patients with afebrile seizures in 70% of cases. In the group of patients with FS, hypersynchronization was observed in 5% of children, while in the group of children with AFS, it was noted in only half of the examined children. Brain MRI changes were observed in 7.5% of patients with FS, and in 25% of patients with AFS.

In the second stage, 60 patients aged 8 to 15 years (average age 11.6±2.35) with a history of febrile seizures, under the observation of a neurologist, were studied.

As a result of examining patients with a history of febrile seizures, we found that the main group had more young children, and the comparison group consisted of older children. The average age in the examined groups was 11.1±2.44 and 12.07±2.18, respectively.

Boys predominated among those examined in both groups, but the difference in the main group was insignificant.

In the main group, more symptomatic forms of epilepsy were found in children (83.3% of examined children). Among them, the shape of the temple prevailed - 46.7% were children.

The genetic burden of febrile seizures was higher in the main group (30%), compared to 20% in the comparison group. Hereditary burden of afebrile seizures was reliably dominant in the main group (36.7%), while in the group with a positive outcome, this indicator was 30% less, equal to 6.7%.

Disturbances during pregnancy were most oFSen noted in patients with epilepsy - 70%, in which gestosis predominated in mothers (53.3%), and XFPN was found in 23.3% of mothers in the main group. Among patients of the comparison group, disorders also prevailed in the antenatal period (46.7%), the leading factor was gestosis (36.7% of children). The intranatal period was disturbed in 31.7% of mothers, which was manifested by weakness in labor activity in the main group, but the difference between the groups was not detected.

As for the timing of childbirth, in this case, it was determined that in 68.3% of the patients we examined, childbirth occurred physiologically and on time. Frailty in labor was the most common, but no significant difference between groups was observed, it was found in 26.7% of mothers in the main group, and 2 times less in the comparison group.

In 51.7% of the children we examined, the onset of febrile seizures corresponded to the age of 1-3 years. We found no difference between the main group and the comparison group. As for the nature of seizures, general seizures with a focal component prevailed in the main group (76.7% of patients), while in the comparison group, on the contrary, generalized seizures were more common (80% of children).

Neurological status disorders were found in 61.7% of examined children. Disturbances in neurostatus were found more oFSen in the main group (96.7%) and they were expressed at a severe level, while in the comparison group focal symptoms were slightly more identified and observed in more than 26% of patients.

Disturbances in the rate of bioelectrical activity of the brain were more reliably detected in children of the main group (80%) than in the comparison group (10%). A similar trend was observed in neuroimaging, where structural changes in the brain were detected more reliably in children in the main group (23.3%), compared to 3.3% of children in the comparison group.

If we take information from the old literature about febrile seizures, as well as their ending, then we can find different, sometimes contradictory opinions. Such a wide range of opinions can be attributed primarily to the fact that there is no single definition of febrile seizures, as well as different approaches to research, patient selection, and study duration.

Current data suggest that febrile seizures are a condition associated with positive quality, age, and heredity [120,157]. However, in up to 30% of cases, febrile seizures are considered the debut variant of some epilepsy syndromes [54,103]. Shorvon et al., (2013), according to some studies[147,167], the probability of febrile seizures progressing to epilepsy ranges from 2% to 7%, depending on the nature of the febrile seizures. According to [46,103], typical forms of febrile seizures change in most cases to either positive-quality focal epilepsy or, in 10-20% of cases, to idiopathic generalized epilepsy [103, 108], in which atypical forms of febrile seizures are symptomatic temporal epilepsy, Dravé syndrome [54], it is also detected at the beginning of myoclonic epilepsy. Other data [158] show that 15–30% of patients with symptomatic temporal lobe epilepsy have atypical forms of febrile seizures.

In a number of cases, the authors [55,110] note the variant status of febrile seizures. In our study, focal forms of epileptic seizures were mainly manifested by atypical febrile seizures (76.7% - common with a focal component, 10% - focal). In 2 patients, febrile seizures progressed to juvenile absence epilepsy, in 2 more cases to childhood epilepsy.

Analyzing the data in the literature, it was found that the main risk factors for the transition of FS to epilepsy are genetic predisposition, premorbid background, as well as the presence of atypical febrile seizures in the anamnesis

[61,118,153,160,162]. is an atypical character of variable seizures. Data from Pavlidou E. et al., (2013) show that only 2% of typical forms of febrile seizures progress to epilepsy, while 4-6% of patients with atypical seizures have a high risk of transition to epilepsy, and 5% in febrile status. According to other sources [111], the risk of progression to epilepsy in complex FSs is 16%–20%. Typical febrile seizures have a 4% chance of becoming afebrile, while atypical febrile seizures have a 92% chance [4].

Based on the data obtained from studies [70,118,133,139,182], it can be said with confidence that genetic weight, complex type of attack, and psycho-neurological disorders are significant factors that increase the risk of febrile seizures becoming afebrile.

According to the results of our work, it can be noted that the genetic factor, focal type of attacks, focal symptoms in neurostatus are predictors of developing epilepsy in patients with FS. In this case, the presence of epilepsy in the family history was more reliably determined in patients with epilepsy (R<0.001), in 76.7% of examined patients with epilepsy, FS had a common character with a focal component, and in 10% - focal character of seizures was determined. In neurostatus, focal symptoms were observed in 53.3% of children, and focal disorders were noted in only 26.7% of patients with a positive result of FS.

EEG cannot be definitively accepted as a risk factor for the transition of febrile seizures to epilepsy, taking into account the different characteristics of the age of patients, as well as the time of onset of seizures [164]. An analysis of some literature data [124,140] showed that no correlation was found between focal phenomena on EEG and the development of afebrile seizures (epilepsy), but some authors [143] reported that the presence of paroxysmal focal phenomena on EEG was more common in patients with FS epilepsy than in patients with a positive outcome. They reported that they were identified 5 times. Sofijanov et al. (1992) found in their study that children with atypical febrile seizures lasting at least 15 minutes had more paroxysmal phenomena on EEG.

Epileptiform paroxysms of focal deceleration type [148] can be observed in febrile status. Other literature data also confirmed that epileptic paroxysms were detected in the EEG of patients with FS, which can be evaluated as a risk factor for the transition of FS to epilepsy [16,33,73,78,126,129,135,183].

On the other hand, the data of Doose H. et al., (2000) emphasize that the presence of epileptiform paroxysms in the electroencephalography of patients under 5 years of age testifies to a predisposition to epilepsy, that is, not as a prognostic factor for the transition of FS to AFS, but to a congenital disorder in the formation of the brain.

In our study, 76.7% of children who ended up with epilepsy had pathology detected in the EEG, while in the group of patients with a positive outcome, this indicator was equal to 3.3%.

Some literature data indicate the influence of structural changes in the brain on the transition of febrile seizures to epilepsy [121,123,151]. Studies on mesial temporal sclerosis are very widespread, for example, some authors [99,109,145] found a difference between the formation of MVS against the background of febrile seizures, other researchers note that febrile seizures occur in only 1-2% of patients with MVS, and H. Holthausen (1997) in his reported that febrile seizures occurred in 18-79% of patients with MVS in their study, and gave generally different data. The problem with these studies is their low follow-up, since at least 5-10 years are required for FS to progress to epilepsy.

Our study showed that 23.3% of children with epilepsy had pathological changes on MRI, while in the comparison group, changes were observed in only 3.3% of children.

Summarizing the above, it is worth noting that genetic predisposition, the presence of focal disturbances in the neurostatus, the presence of a focal component in an attack can be considered as an open prognostic factor of the risk of transitioning to an afebrile form of FS, while the pathological changes identified in neurophysiological research methods are risk factors that increase this possibility.

Data from the literature on the studies conducted confirm that typical FS does not have psycho-speech disorders. At the same time, it is important to mention that even one episode of FS occurs very oFSen in children who have experienced perinatal damage to the nervous system. We can certainly associate the delay in psycho-verbal development with PPNS in typical FS. Prolonged and repeated FS can lead to atrophy of the hippocampus, and an increase in the number of FS attacks can cause a delay in psycho-speech development and negatively affect the formation of cognitive status [28,30]. In most cases, children with FS have memory and attention deficits, as well as rapid fatigue in any type of physical and mental load, oFSen these are hyperactive emotionally labile children who are difficult to control and manage [12]. Early onset, multiple repetitions and long duration of FS affect not only the development of speech, the formation of auditory-speech memory, but also lead to motor side effects in these children [30].

Treatment and management of patients with FS receive considerable attention in the literature. According to the authors, complex therapy using nootropic drugs in young doses is recognized depending on the somatic condition of the body [5,15,36,37]. It is also very important to correct psycho-speech disorders in atypical FS. According to the authors of the study, the correction of psycho-speech disorders should be implemented comprehensively [26,27,30,44,74,75]. It is necessary to include a course of drugs, training with a speech therapist and a speech therapist, as well as to correct the instability of micro- and macroelements [3,11,12,13,14,36,66]. Activities with children in a comfortable environment and in the form of games are recommended. It is very important for parents to communicate with their children, mostly in the same language, because this is one of the elements of correction [44,45]. In recent years, methods of stimulation therapy - micropolarization method, transcranial magnetic stimulation method have become very popular [34,44,45], which improves the effect of complex correction.

We used several methods to assess neuropsychological development, taking into account the different age groups of the children we examined. To examine children under 5 years of age, we used the Denver psychomotor development test, and to study children with a history of FS, we used the Wechsler intelligence test (WISC – Wechsler Intelligence Scale for Children) and L.I. Wassermana, E.D. Khomskoy, L.S. Tsvetkovoy, A.B. Partially modified using the methods of Semenovich, traditional A.R. We used a battery of Lurie tests.

As for individual indicators of the Denver test, we found a difference between the groups. Among the patients, more fine motor disorders (61.7%) were observed, which was found in the group with more afebrile seizures (75% of children), while in the TFS and ATFS group, it was 50% and 60% of children, respectively.

Combining the data of the Denver scale, we distinguished 3 types of psychomotor development: normative, speech development and delay of fine motor skills, general delay of psychomotor development (Fig. Analysis of the data of the Denver scale showed that in the group with typical febrile seizures, 7 (35%) patients had speech development and fine motor delay, and 5 (25%) children had general developmental delay. In the group with atypical febrile seizures, 40% of patients had a delay in speech development and fine motor skills in hands. The most pronounced changes were noted in the group with afebrile seizures, where 35% of children had a delay in general development, 40% of children had a delay in speech development and fine motor skills, and only 25% of patients were assessed as developmentally normal.

Later, we conducted a neuropsychological study in children with FS, and in the anamnesis we used the Wechsler intelligence test (WISC – Wechsler Intelligence Scale for Children) and A.R. We used Lurii's modified battery of tests.

Overall, children with FS transitioned to epilepsy scored lower than children with a positive outcome, as expected, and verbal intelligence scores were nonsignificantly higher than nonverbal intelligence scores. In a study of nonverbal intelligence in patients with FS transitioning to epilepsy, children with FSE had the greatest problems with tests of coordination and attention, a scrambling test, and tests of putting parts together, as in verbal intelligence.

When verbal intelligence was studied in patients with epilepsy, small difficulties were observed in tests of vocabulary, where it was necessary to identify concepts and explain the meaning of words, and in tests of similarity, in which children had problems with identifying and distinguishing objects by some common features. Children performed the awareness and comprehension tests easily.

Then, A.R. We have conducted a comprehensive neuropsychological study of Lurie's modified complex tests.

Examination of motor functions in children with good-quality febrile seizures showed that 23.3% of children had mild impairments, so that, for example, the test using the piano, its reverse order, caused difficulties for the examinees, in particular, these children performed a sequence of movements. they made mistakes. Also, graphic tests in these children led to difficulties, namely, an increase in the time spent on performing tasks, a violation of the sequence of objects.

Children with FS progression to epilepsy had significantly more and more severe psychoneurological disorders. In total, disorders were detected in 26 (86.7%) children, and only 4 had a normal variant.

Thus, the study of psycho-speech disorders in patients with a history of febrile seizures showed that when the disease progresses to afebrile paroxysms, there is a delay in mental and psycho-speech development. this requires the maximum early involvement of not only medication, but also cognitive correction methods.

FS correct treatment and preventive algorithm for children

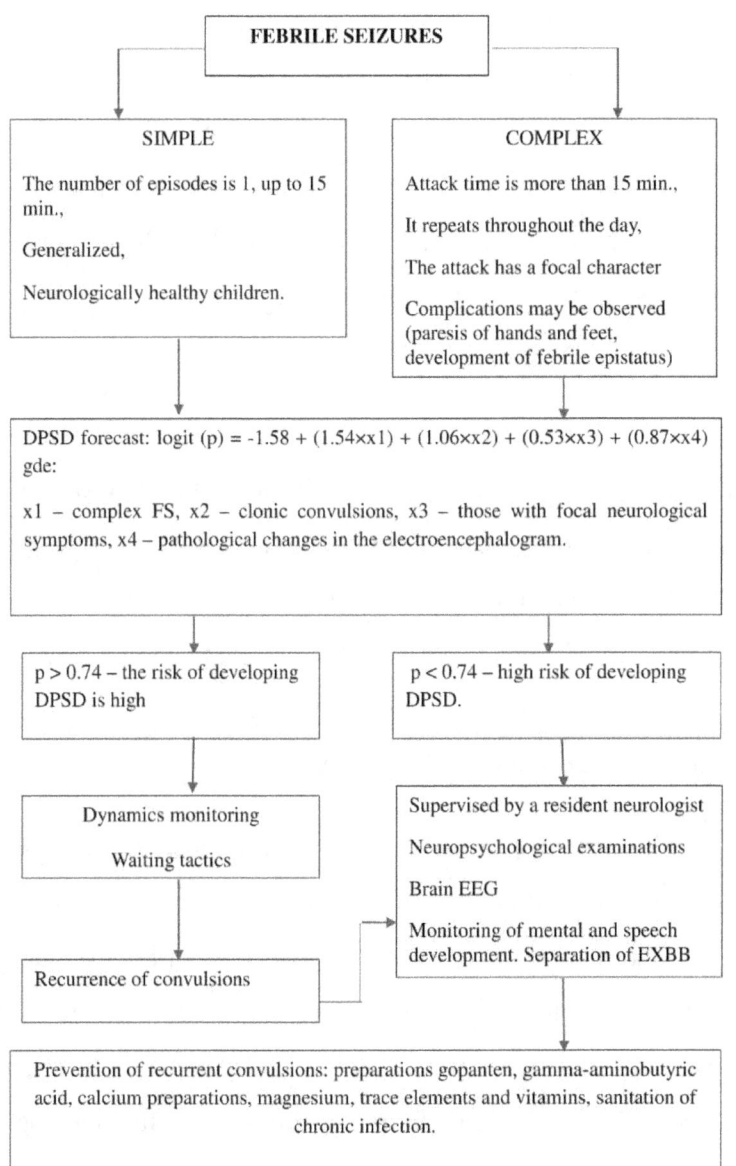

CONCLUSIONS:

1. The risk factors for febrile seizures and their recurrence are genetic predisposition to febrile seizures (35%), perinatal damage to the central nervous system in the anamnesis (75%) and frequent respiratory diseases (55%). The risk factors for the transformation of febrile seizures into epilepsy include hereditary predisposition to epilepsy (36.7%), focal nature of febrile seizures (76.7%) and the presence of organic neurological symptoms (80%).

2. Typical (ordinary) febrile seizures in terms of clinical course were characterized by scattered microorganism signs (50%) and absence of epileptic patterns in the post-seizure EEG. In atypical (complex) febrile seizures, focal signs were observed in 75% of cases. Various changes in the EEG examination and neuroimaging examinations revealed structural changes in the brain in 15% of patients.

3. In neuropsychological examinations, in cases where febrile seizures transformed into epilepsy in the anamnesis, speech and mental development was delayed in 86.7%, auditory and verbal memory disorders were found in 73.3%, and it was determined that it depends on the number and duration of seizures. Simple one-time febrile seizures were distinguished by the age-appropriateness of mental and seizure development.

4. According to the new tactics of providing medical care to children with FS, it is carried out taking into account all identified risk factors. Diagnosis of FS should be based on differential approaches.

REFERENCES:

1. Абдурахимов А., Умарова М., Абдунабиева Х. Антропометрические показатели физического развития детей: Монография

2. Алимова Х. П. Принципы неотложной помощи при фебрильных судорогах у детей: научное издание / // Вестник экстренной медицины. - Ташкент, 2017. - Том XI N3. - С. 74-78.

3. Аханькова Т. Е. Социально-демографические и эмоционально-коммуникативные характеристики родителей и их детей с нарушениями речевого развития: научное издание / Т. Е. Аханькова, К. М. Шипкова // Российский психиатрический журнал: научно-практический журнал / Основан в 1997 году. - Москва: ФГБУ "НМИЦПН им В. П. Сербского" Минздрава России. - 2019. - N 6. - С. 45-47.

4. Бадалян, Л.О. Фебрильные судороги: диагностика, лечение, диспансерное наблюдение : метод. рек. / Л.О. Бадалян, П.А. Темин, К.Ю. Мухин. – Москва, 1988. – 24 с.

5. Белоусова Е. Д. Фебрильные судороги: что о них должны знать педиатры: научное издание / Е. Д. Белоусова // Российский вестник перинатологии и педиатрии. - 2018. - Том 63 N6. - С. 108-114.

6. Бобылова М.Ю., Некрасова И.В., Ильина Е.С., Кваскова Н.В. Миоклонус у детей: дефиниции и классификации, дифференциальный диагноз, принципы терапии (лекция) // Рус. журн. детской неврологии. - 2014. - Т. 9, № 2. - С. 32-41.

7. Броун Т.Р., Холмс Г.Л. Эпилепсия. Клиническое руководство, Фебрильные судороги. В кн.: Педиатрия. Под ред. Баранова А.А.

8. Вассерман Л.И., Дорофеева С.А., Меерсон Я.А., Трауготт Н.Н. Стандартизованный набор диагностических нейропсихологических методик: Методические рекомендации. Л., 1987. 55 с.,

9. Вашура, Л. В. Судорожные приступы у детей с герпесвирусными инфекциями: дифференциальная диагностика и исходы: автореф. дис. .канд. мед. наук: 14.01.08, 14.01. - М., 2016. - 28 с.

10. Войтенков В.Б., Скрипченко Н.В. фебрильные судороги при инфекционных заболеваниях у детей и их нейрофизиологическая характеристика 2012

11. Волкова С. В. Вариативные технологии преодоления фонематических расстройств у детей с речевыми нарушениями, обусловленными органическим поражением головного мозга различного генеза: научное издание / С. В. Волкова // Дефектология. - М., 2015. - N5. - С. 82-91.

12. Волковская Т. Н. Коммуникативный подход в контексте современной методологии психолого-педагогической помощи детям с недостатками речевого развития: научное издание / Т. Н. Волковская, И. Ю. Левченко // Дефектология: научно-методический журнал / Российская академия образования, Институт коррекционной педагогики РАО. - Москва: ООО "Школьная Пресса". - 2020. - N 3. - С. 17-21.

13. Голубева В. Ю. [и др.] Задержка психического и речевого развития у детей - этапы оказания специализированной помощи: Тезисы XIX Российского конгресса «Инновационные технологии в педиатрии и детской хирургии» с международным участием (Москва, 20-22 октября 2020 г.) / // Российский вестник перинатологии и педиатрии: научно-практический рецензируемый журнал / ООО "Национальная педиатрическая академия науки и инноваций", Некоммерческая организация "Российская ассоциация педиатрических центров". - Москва: "Оверлей". - 2020. - Том 65 N 4 (Часть 1). - С. 290

14. Грибова О. Е. Психолого-педагогическая диагностика детей с речевыми нарушениями: проблемные аспекты в подготовке специалистов. Часть 2: научное издание / О. Е. Грибова, Е. Л. Инденбаум // Дефектология: научно-методический журнал / Российская академия

образования, Институт коррекционной педагогики РАО. - Москва: ООО "Школьная Пресса". - 2020. - N 5. - С. 22-32.

15. Гузева В. И. Исследование терапевтического влияния гопантеновой кислоты (пантогама) у детей с эпилепсией и речевыми нарушениями: научное издание / В. И. Гузева, В. В. Гузева [и др.] // Педиатрия. Журнал имени Г. Н. Сперанского. - М., 2015. - Том 94 N3. - С. 148-157.

16. Гузева, Е.И. Пароксизмальные расстройства сознания у детей раннего возраста (диагностика и реабилитация): автореф. дис. ... д-ра мед. наук / Е.И. Гузева. – Санкт-Петербург, 1992. – 37 с.

17. Делягин В. М.Лихорадка. Многообразие причин и сложность решения // № 1 (93) – I/II 2013 г. : Лікарю-практику.

18. Джубатова Р. С. и соавт. Эффективность неотложных мероприятий при фебрильных судорогах у детей: научное издание // Материалы пятого съезда Анестезиологов-Реаниматологов Узбекистана с Международным участием (г. Ташкент, 8-9 июня 2017 год). - Ташкент, 2017. - С. 204

19. Дмитренко Д.В., Шнайдер Н.А., Мартынова Г.П., Строганова М.А. и др. Мутации натриевых каналов как генетический предиктор фебрильных приступов у детей // Современные проблемы науки и образования. 2015. № 5;

URL: www.science-education.ru/128-22774. — Москва, Академия естествознания, 2015

20. Доклад Президента Шавката Мирзиёева на торжественном собрании, посвященном 26-летию принятия Конституции Республики Узбекистан от 08.12.2018.

21. Долинина А.Ф Факторы риска трансформации фебрильных судорог в эпилепсию. Неврология, нейропсихиатрия, психосоматика 2015 (спецвыпуск 1) 22-25)

22. Долинина А.Ф., Громова Л.Л., Мухин К.Ю. Факторы риска рецидива фебрильных судорог 2015 г. Эпилепсия и пароксзизмальные состояния №1 том7, 20-24

23. Долинина, Антонина Федоровна Фебрильные судороги - диагностика, тактика медицинской помощи и прогноз : автореферат дис. ... доктора медицинских наук : 14.01.11 Москва 2016

24. Дорофеева, Наталья Евгеньевна Особенности когнитивных функций у детей школьного возраста с идиопатическими формами эпилепсии : диссертация ... кандидата медицинских наук : 14.01.11 Санкт-Петербург 2011

25. Захарова Т. В. Создание модели изучения и формирования социальных эмоций как условия успешной социализации детей с речевыми нарушениями в условиях инклюзивного образования: научное издание / Т. В.

Захарова, А. А. Моисеева // Дефектология. - М., 2014. - N5. - С. 51-64.

26. Зияходжаева Л. У. Состояние когнитивных функций у детей с фебрильными судорогами: научное издание / Л. У. Зияходжаева // Неврология. - Ташкент, 2012. - N3-4. - С. 154-155

27. Инденбаум Е. Л. Психолого-педагогическая диагностика детей с речевыми нарушениями: проблемные аспекты в подготовке специалистов. Часть I: научное издание / Е. Л. Инденбаум, О. Е. Грибова // Дефектология: научно-методический журнал / Российская академия образования, Институт коррекционной педагогики РАО. - Москва: ООО "Школьная Пресса". - 2020. - N 4. - С. 20-31.

28. Исмаилова М. А. Динамика качественной оценки развития детей до года: научное издание / М. А. Исмаилова, Р. С. Джубатова, С. Е. Куркова // Инфекция, иммунитет и фармакология. - Ташкент, 2011. - №8. - С. 44-48.

29. Исмаилова Н.Б. Исходы фебрильных судорог у детей. 13 марта 2013. УДК:616.8–009.2–053.2

30. Ишанходжаева Г. Т. Характеристика речевых нарушений у детей перенесших острый менингоэнцефалит: тезисы конференции "Актуальные проблемы неврологии", посвященной 90-летию академика Н. М. Маджидова (Ташкент, 14 декабря 2018 г.) / Г. Т. Ишанходжаева //

Nevrologiya: рецензируемый научно-практический журнал / Министерство здравоохранения Республики Узбекистан, Ассоциация неврологов Республики Узбекистан. - Ташкент: ООО "Printmedia". - 2019. - N 4 (Часть 2). - С. 158

31. Калюжная Л.И., Земляной Д.А. Нарушение теплообмена и лихорадка. Педиатр том 6 №1 2015г

32. Китаева В.Е. Котов А.С. Серия пациентов с фебрильным эпилептическим статусом: клинические проявления и долгосрочный катамнез. Русский журнал детской неврологии 2020 15(1): 28-39

33. Ковеленова, М.В. Фебрильные судороги : автореф. дис. ... канд. мед. наук / М.В. Ковеленова. – Санкт-Петербург, 1996. – 26 с.

34. Кузнецова Е. Задержка речевого развития: нейрофизиологический подход: научное издание / Е. Кузнецова // Врач. - М., 2017. - N8. - С. 47-50

35. Кураматов Ш. Ю. Неотложная терапия фебрильных судорог у детей: научное издание / Ш. Ю. Кураматов, Х. Х. Холматов, Х. М. Юлчиев, Р. Я. Рахмонов // Вестник экстренной медицины. - Ташкент, 2014. - N2. - С. 12-13

36. Лазебник Т. А. Коррекция речевых нарушений у детей дошкольного возраста: научное издание / Т. А. Лазебник, В. Н. Румянцева [и др.] // Medical express. - Ташкент, 2012. - №1. - С. 44-47

37. Ларькина Е. В. Тактика ведения детей дошкольного возраста с различными вариантами задержки речевого развития: научное издание / Е. В. Ларькина, О. В. Халецкая // Журнал неврологии и психиатрии имени С.С. Корсакова. - М., 2014. - Том 114 N2. - С. 94-98.

38. Литвицкий П.Ф. Общая этиология расстройств нервной деятельности. Нейрогенные патологические синдромы Вопросы современной педиатрии. 2013;12(4):73-90. https://doi.org/10.15690/vsp.v12i4.734 38

39. Лоурин М.И. Лихорадка у детей. Пер. с англ. М.: Медицина, 1985; 255

40. Лурия А.Р. Основы нейропсихологии: Учебное пособие. М., 1973. 176 с., 36

41. Лурия А.Р. Функциональная организация мозга // Естественно-научные основы психологии. 1978. С. 109-140

42. Маджидова Ё. Н. Клиническая и нейрофизиологическая (вызванные потенциалы мозга) оценка умеренных когнитивных расстройств у больных с хронической ишемией мозга: научное издание // Неврология. - Ташкент, 2013. - N2. - С. 5-8.

43. Маджидова Ё. Н. Микротоковая рефлексотерапия в реабилитации детей с последствием ППНС задержкой психо-речевого развития: Тезисы

конференции "Актуальные проблемы неврологии", посвященной 90-летию академика Н. М. Маджидова (Ташкент, 14 декабря 2018 г.) / Ё. Н. Маджидова, Г. У. Рашидова, И. Р. Насирова // Nevrologiya. - Ташкент, 2018. - N4. - С. 117

44. Маджидова Ё. Н. Роль методов микротоковой рефлексотерапии в реабилитации детей с задержкой психо-речевого развития: тезисы конференции "Актуальные проблемы неврологии", посвященной 90-летию академика Н. М. Маджидова (Ташкент, 14 декабря 2018 г.) / Ё. Н. Маджидова, Г. У. Рашидова, С. А. Усманов // Nevrologiya: рецензируемый научно-практический журнал / Министерство здравоохранения Республики Узбекистан, Ассоциация неврологов Республики Узбекистан. - Ташкент: ООО "Printmedia". - 2019. - N 4 (Часть 2). - С. 160

45. Маджидова Ё.Н., Азимова Н.М. Клинико-неврологическая характеристика детей с речевыми нарушениями: Тезисы конференции "Актуальные проблемы неврологии", посвященной 90-летию академика Н. М. Маджидова (Ташкент, 14 декабря 2018 г.) / Н. М. Азимова [и др.] // Nevrologiya. - Ташкент, 2018. - N4. - С. 111

46. Мартынова, Г. П. Эпидемиология фебрильных приступов в детской популяции города Красноярска / Г. П. Мартынова, Н. А. Шнайдер, М. А.

47. Медведев, М. И. Проблемы диагностики и терапии судорожных состояний в раннем детском возрасте и пути их решения / М. И. Медведев // Педиатрия. - 2012. - Т. 91, № 3. - С. 149-158.

48. Минько А. Г. Фебрильные судороги у детей раннего возраста

49. Миронов М. Б., Т. М. Красильщикова, Д. Н. Смирнов, М. Ю. Бобылова, И. О. Щедеркина, С. Г. Бурд, Т. Т. Батышева. Клинический случай новорожденного с оро-букко-лингвальными приступами. Сибирское медицинское обозрение. 2017; (1): 77-81. DOI: 10.20333/2500136-2017-1-77-81

50. Миронов, М.Б. Исходы и трансформация фебрильных приступов у детей по данным института детской неврологии и эпилепсии имени Святителя Луки / М.Б. Миронов, К.Ю. Мухин // Русский журн. детской неврологии. – 2012. – No7(4). – С. 3-16.

51. Муратов Ф. Х. Фебрильные судороги как предиктор эпилепсии: научное издание / Ф. Х. Муратов, М. А. Абдурахманова // Nevrologiya. - Ташкент, 2017. - Том 701 N2. - С. 41-42.

52. Мусабекова Т. О., Хамзина А. И., Андрианова Е.В. Фебрильные судороги у детей, клинико-вегетативные особенности // Вестник Казахского Национального медицинского университета, 2014

53. Мухамедханова Н. Б. Изучение дерматоглифических особенностей в дифференциальной диагностике фебрильных приступов: научное издание / Н. Б. Мухамедханова, М. С. Гильдиева // Nevrologiya. - Ташкент, 2017. - Том 70 N2. - С. 24-25.

54. Мухин, К.Ю. Палеокортикальная височная эпилепсия, обусловленная мезиальным височным склерозом: клиника, диагностика и лечение (обзор литературы) / К.Ю. Мухин, С.Х. Гатауллина, А.С. Петрухин // Русский журн. детской неврологии. – 2008. – Т.3, No3. – С. 41-60.

55. Мухин, К.Ю. Тяжелая миоклоническая эпилепсия младенчества / К.Ю. Мухин, П.А. Темин, М.Ю. Никанорова [и др.] // Журн. неврологии и психиатрии. – 1997. – Т.97, No8. – С. 61-64.

56. Мухин, К.Ю. Фебрильные приступы (лекция) / К.Ю. Мухин, М.Б. Миронов, А.Ф. Долинина [и др.] // Русский журн. детской неврологии. – 2010. – Т. 5, Вып. 2. – С. 17-30.

57. Мухин, К.Ю. Электроэнцефалографические изменения при синдроме Драве / К.Ю. Мухин, О.А. Пылаева, М.Б. Миронов [и др.] // Русский журн. детской неврологии. – 2014. – No4. – С. 6-13.

58. Никольский М.А. Сероконверсия и нарастание концентрации IgG-антител при инфекции,

вызванной вирусом герпеса человека 6-го типа у детей: научное издание / М. А. Никольский, В. Г. Мессорош, С. И. Минченко // Эпидемиология и инфекционные болезни. - Москва, 2011. - №3. - С. 15-18.

59. Никольский, М. А. Роль вирусов герпеса человека 6 и 7-го типов в возникновении фебрильных судорог у детей / М. А. Никольский, М. В. Радыш // Вопр. диагностики и педиатрии. - 2012. - Т. 4, № 4. - С. 46-48.

60. Олимов А. Р. Особенности течения фебрильных судорог у детей на госпитальном этапе: научное издание / А. Р. Олимов, М. А. Ахматалиева // Вестник экстренной медицины. - Ташкент, 2014. - N2. - С. 186

61. Петрухин, А.С. Фебрильные судороги / А.С. Петрухин // Эпилептология детского возраста / А.С. Петрухин, К.Ю. Мухин, Н.К. Благосклонова [и др.]. – Москва: Медицина, 2000. – С. 279-284.

62. Пилипец, Е.Ю. Применение диакарба в лечении детей с эпилепсией и фебрильными судорогами / Е.Ю. Пилипец, Л.Н. Танцура // Врачебное дело. – 2005. – No5. – С. 73-76.

63. Рахимова С.Р., Мирзаева А.Д., Курбанова Р.Р., Акбаева Н.А. Клинические аспекты фебрильных судорог// emergence medicine (неотложная медицина) issn 2409-563x. medicus. 2021. № 4 (40).

64. Семенович А.В., Архипов Б.А. Методологические аспекты нейропсихологической диагностики отклоняющегося развития // Проблемы специальной психологии и психодиагностики отклоняющегося развития.1998. С 54.-75.]

65. Скрипченко, Н.В. Гетерогенность судорожного синдрома при инфекционных заболеваниях у детей / Н.В. Скрипченко, Е.М. Кривошеенко, В.Н. Команцев [и др.] // Рос. вестн. перинатологии и педиатрии. – 2012. – Т.57, №6. – С. 50-58.

66. Солиева М.Ю Физическое развитие детей младшего школьного возраста // Архив исследований АГМИ, 27 мая 2021.

67. Стенина, О.И. Этиология и структура судорожного синдрома у детей первых двух лет жизни / О.И. Стенина, А.К. Углицких, С.С. Паунова // Педиатрия. Журнал им. Г.Н. Сперанского. – 2013. – Т. 92, №1. – С. 77-83.

68. Строганова М. А. 1, Г. П. Мартынова1, Н. А. Шнайдер1, А. А. Колодина2 Структура вирусных триггеров фебрильных приступов у детей раннего возраста ГБОУ ВПО Красноярский государственный медицинский университ Детские инфекции №3 2016 год

69. Строганова М.А., Шнайдер Н.А., Мартынова Г.П., Дюжакова А.В. Фебрильные приступы у детей // Справочник врача общей практики. 2014. №12. С.47—55.

70. Строганова М.А., Шнайдер Н.А., Мартынова Г.П., Дюжакова А.В. Эпидемиология фебрильных приступов (обзор) // В мире научных открытий. – 2014. – Т. 56, № 8. – С. 216– 231

71. Студеникин, В. М. Эпилепсия и судорожные синдромы у детей / В. М. Студеникин // Лечащий врач. - 2014. - № 10. - С. 61-64.

72. Студеникин, В.М. Фебрильные судороги / В.М. Студеникин, В.И. Шелковский, С.В. Балканская // Практика педиатра. – 2007. – No1. – С. 8- 10.

73. Трепилец, В.М. Простые фебрильные судороги в практике педиатра и детского невролога : особенности течения и риск развития эпилепсии / В.М. Трепилец, Г.С. Голосная, И.О. Щедеркина [и др.] // Педиатрия. Журн. им. Г.Н. Сперанского. – 2014. – Т.93, No1. – С. 65-67.

74. Туровская Н.Г. Об актуальности выявления особенностей психического развития детей, перенесших в анамнезе судорожные пароксизмальные состояния // Экспериментальные методики патопсихологии и опыт их применения (к 100-летию С.Я.Рубинштейн)

75. Туровская Н.Г. Психическое развитие детей дошкольного возраста с судорожными состояниями Автореф. дисс канд. мед. наук. С-П., 2013.

76. Указ президента республики узбекистан о комплексных мерах по коренному совершенствованию системы здравоохранения республики узбекистан от 07.12.2018.

77. Указ президента республики узбекистан о мерах по кардинальному совершенствованию системы государственной поддержки лиц с инвалидностью от 04.12.2017

78. Фебрильные припадки и генерализованная эпилепсия с фебрильными припадками плюс // Карлов, В.А. Эпилепсия у детей и взрослых женщин и мужчин : рук. для врачей / В.А. Карлов. – Москва : Медицина, 2010. – С. 162-166.

79. Фебрильные судороги. В кн.: Педиатрия. Под ред. Баранова А.А. (Серия: «Клинические рекомендации»). М.: ГЭОТАР-МЕДИА, 2009; 349–59.,

80. Хамзина А.И. Особенности ВНС у детей с фебрильными судорогами и эпилепсией // Медицина Кыргызстана №4 2012

81. Хамзина А.И фебрильные приступы у детей. современные аспекты.дефиниции, классификации, патогенеза и лечения

82. Хомская Е.Д. Хрестоматия по нейропсихологии. М., 1999. 265с.,

83. Чутко Л. С. Последствия специфических расстройств речевого развития у детей: научное издание / Л. С. Чутко, С. Ю. Сурушкина [и др.] // Журнал неврологии и психиатрии имени С. С. Корсакова. - М., 2018. - Том 118 N5. - С. 54-57.

84. Шамансуров Ш. Ш. Изучения уровня аутоантител к фактору роста нервов у детей с задержкой психомоторного и речевого развития / Ш. Ш. Шамансуров, Д. Н. Гулямова, Н. Е. Абдушукурова // Журнал теоретической и клинической медицины. - Ташкент, 2011. - N7. - С. 89-91

85. Шамансуров Ш. Ш. Роль перинатальных факторов и наследственности в развитии фебрильных судорог / Ш. Ш. Шамансуров, Н. А. Мирсаидова, Н. М. Абдукадирова // Неврология. - Ташкент, 2010. - N3. - С. 56-58.

86. Шамансуров Ш. Ш. Электроэнцефалографические исследования у детей с задержкой психомоторного и речевого развития / Ш. Ш. Шамансуров, Н. М. Зиямухамедова, Ч. А. Узакова, Г. С. Халимбетов // Российский вестник перинатологии и педиатрии. - М., 2011. - N4. - С. 88-89.

87. Шамансуров, Ш.Ш. Наследственный фактор у детей с фебрильными конвульсиями / Ш.Ш. Шамансуров, Н.А. Мирсаидова, Н.М. Абдукадырова // Врач-аспирант. – 2010. – Т. 39, No2.1. – С. 189-194.

88. Шевкетова Л.Ш. Приоритеты оказания экстренной помощи на догоспитальном этапе детям раннего возраста с фебрильными судорогами: научное издание / Л. Ш. Шевкетова, Б. С. Рахимов, Д. А. Рахимова, М. К. Мухитдинова // Вестник экстренной медицины. - Ташкент, 2010. - №3. - С. 150-151

89. Шелковский, В.И. Проблема фебрильных судорог у детей / В.И. Шелковский, В.М. Студеникин, О.И. Маслова [и др.] // Вопр. современной педиатрии. – 2005. – Т.4, No4. – С. 50-53.

90. Шнайдер Н.А., Шаповалова Е.А., Дмитренко Д.В., Садыкова А.В., Шаповалова Л.П. Эпидемиология детской эпилепсии // Сибирское медицинское обозрение. – 2012. – Т.74, №2. – С. 44-50.

91. Ягунова К. В. Унифицированный подход к диагностике и раннему выявлению речевых нарушений у детей: научное издание / К. В. Ягунова, Д. Д. Гайнетдинова // Неврологический вестник журнал имени В. М. Бехтерева. - Казань, 2018. - Том L N2. - С. 110-111.

92. Abou-Khalil, B. Familial genetic predisposition, epilepsy localization and antecedent febrile seizures / B. Abou-

Khalil, L. Krei, B. Lazenby [et al.] // Epilepsy Res. – 2007. – Vol.73, No1. – P. 104-110.

93. Aicardi J. Diseases of the nervous system in children. 3rd ed. London. Mac Keith Press/Distributed by Wiley-Blackwell. 2009; 966

94. Aicardi, J. Febrile convulsions / J. Aicardi // Epilepsy in Children. – New York : Raven Press, 1994. – P. 253-275.

95. Airede, A.I. Febrile convulsions : Factors and recurrence rate / A.I. Airede // Trop. Gcogr. Med. – 1992. – Vol. 44. – P. 233-237.

96. Al-Eissa, Y.A. Febrile seizures : Rate and risk factors of recurrence / Y.A. Al- Eissa // J. Child Neurol. – 1995. – Vol. 10. – P. 315-319.

97. Annegers, J.F. Recurrence risk of febrile convulsions in a population-based cohort / J.F. Annegers, S.A. Blakely, W.A. Hauser [et al.] // Epilepsy Res. –1990. – Vol. 5, No3. – P. 209-216.

98. Arzimanoglou, A. Aicardi's epilepsy in children / A. Arzimanoglou, R. Guerrini, J. Aicardi. – 3-rd edition. – Lippincott, Philadelphia, 2004. – 516 p.

99. Asadi-Pooya, A.A. Comparison of temporal lobe epilepsy with hippocampal sclerosis and temporal lobe epilepsies due to other etiologies / A.A. Asadi- Pooya, M.

Tajvarpour, B. Vedadinezhad [et al.] // Med J Islam Repub Iran. – 2015. – Vol. 29. – P. 263.

100. Assogba, K. Febrile seizures in one-five aged infants in tropical practice : Frequency, etiology and outcome of hospitalization / K. Assogba, B. Balaka, F.A. Touglo [et al.] // J Pediatr Neurosci. – 2015. – Vol. 10, No1. – P. 9-12.

101. Baldin, E. Prevalence of recurrent symptoms and their association with epilepsy and febrile seizure in school-aged children: a community-based survey in Iceland / E. Baldin, P. Ludvigsson, O. Mixa [et al.] // Epilepsy Behav. -2012. - Vol. 23, № 3. - P. 315-319.

102. Baum L., Haerian B.S., Ng H.K., Wong V.C., Ng P.W., Lui C.H., Sin N.C., Zhang C., Tomlinson B., Wong G.W., Tan H.J., Raymond A.A., Mohamed Z., Kwan P. Case-control association study of polymorphisms in the voltage-gated sodium channel genes SCN1A, SCN2A, SCN3A, SCN1B, and SCN2B and epilepsy// Human genetics. – 2014. – Vol. 133, № 5. – P. 651- 659. . M. .

103. Berg, A.T. Childhood-onset epilepsy with and without preceding febrile seizures / A.T. Berg, S. Shinnar, S.R. Levy [et al.] // Neurology. – 1999. – Vol. 53. – P. 1742-1748.

104. Berg, A.T. Predictors of recurrent febrile seizures: A prospective cohort study / A.T. Berg, S. Shinnar, A.S. Darefsky [et al.] // Arch. Pediatr. Adolesc. Med. – 1997. – Vol. 151. – P. 371-378.

105. Berg, A.T. Recurrent Febrile Seizures / A.T. Berg // Febrile Seizures / ed.: T.Z. Baram, S. Shinnar. – San Diego [etc.] : Academic press, 2002. – P. 37-52.

106. Berg, A.T. Risk factors for a first febrile seizure : A matched case-control study / A.T. Berg, S. Shinnar, E.D. Shapiro [et al.] // Epilepsia. – 1995. – Vol. 36. – P. 334-341.

107. Camfield, P. Antecedents and Risk Factors for Febrile Seizures / P. Camfield, C. Camfield, K. Gordon // Febrile Seizures / ed.: T.Z. Baram, S. Shinnar. – San Diego [etc.] : Academic press, 2002. – P. 27-36.

108. Camfield, P. What types of epilepsy are preceded by febrile seizures? A population-based study of children / P. Camfield, C. Camfield, K. Gordon [et al.] // Dev. Med. Child Neurol. – 1994. – Vol. 36. – P. 887-892.

109. Camfield, P.R. Febrile Seizures and Genetics Epilepsy with Febrile Seizures plus (GEFS+) / P.R. Camfield, C.S. Camfield, I.E. Scheffer [et al.] // Epileptic syndromes in infancy, childhood and adolescence. – 5th ed. – United Kingdom :John Libbey Eurotext, 2012. – P. 175-187.

110. Ceulemans, B. Severe myoclonic epilepsy in infancy: toward an optimal treatment / B. Ceulemans, M. Boel, L. Claes [et al.] // J. Child Neurology. – 2004. – Vol.19. – P. 516-521.

111. Chungath, M. The mortality and morbidity offebrile seizures / M. Chungath, S. Shorvon // Nat Clin Pract Neurol. – 2008. – Vol. 4, No11. – P. 610-621.

112. Doose, H. The concept of hereditary impairment of brain maturation / H. Doose, B.A. Neubauer, B. Petersen // Epileptic Disorders. – 2000. – Vol.2, Suppl.1. – P. 45-49.

113. Dravet, Ch. Dravet syndrome / Ch. Dravet, R. Guerrini. – France, Paris : John Libbey, 2011. – 120 p.

114. El-Radhi, A.S. Recurrence rate of febrile convulsion related to the degree of pyrexia during the first attack / A.S. El-Radhi, K. Withana, S. Banejeh // Clin. Pediatr. – 1986. – Vol. 25. – P. 311-313.

115. Ellatiff, A. Risk factors of febrile disease among preschool children in Alexandria / A. Ellatiff, H. Garawamy // Journal of the Egyptian Public Health Association. – 2002. – Vol. 77, No1-2. – P. 156-172.

116. Elshana, H. A tertiary care center's experience with febrile seizures: Evaluation of 632cases / H. Elshana, M. Özmen, T. Aksu Uzunhan [et al.] // Minerva Pediatr. – 2015. – Jun 4. – [Epub ahead of print].

117. Eseigbe E.E., S.J. Adama, P. Eseigbe // Niger Med J. - 2012. - Vol. 53, №3. - P. 140-144.

118. Fallah, R. Afebrile seizure subsequent to initial febrile seizure / R. Fallah, S. Akhavan Karbasi, M. Golestan // Singapore Med J. – 2012. – Vol. 53, No 5. – P. 349-352.

119. Fallah, R. Recurrence of febrile seizure in Yazd, Iran / R. Fallah, S.A. Karbasi // Turk J Pediatr. – 2010. – Vol. 52, No 6. – P. 618-22.

120. Febrile seizures: Consensus development conference summary // National Institutes of Health. – Bethesda, MD, 1980. – Vol. 3, No2. – P. 1-10.

121. Feng, B. Generation of Febrile Seizures and Subsequent Epileptogenesis / B. Feng, Z. Chen // Neurosci Bull. – 2016. – Aug 25. – [Epub ahead of print].

122. Fenichel, G.M. Neurological complications of immunization / G.M. Fenichel // Ann Neurol. – 1982. – No12. – P. 119-128.

123. Finegersh, A. Bilateral hippocampal atrophy in temporal lobe epilepsy: Effect of depressive symptoms and febrile seizures / A. Finegersh, C. Avedissian, S. Shamim [et al.] // Epilepsia. – 2011. – Vol. 52, No4. – P. 689-697.

124. Frantzen, E. Longitudinal EEC and clinical study of children with febrile convulsions / E. Frantzen, M. Lennox-Buchthal, A. Nygaard// Electroencephalogr. Clin. Neurophysiol. – 1968. – Vol. 24. – P. 197-212.

125. Gohnston, M.V. Febrile seizures / M.V. Gohnston // Nelson Textbook of Pediatrics / eds. R.M. Kliegman, R.E. Behrman, H.B. Jenson [et al.]. – Philadelphia, USA : Sunders, 2007. – P. 2459-2458.

126. Gradisnik, P. Predictive value of paroxysmal EEG abnormalities for future epilepsy in focal febrile seizures / P. Gradisnik, B. Zagradisnik, M. Palfy [et al.] // Brain Dev. – 2015. – Vol. 37, No9. – P. 868-873.

127. Graves, R.C. Febrile seizures: risks, evaluation, and prognosis / R.C. Graves, K. Oehler, L.E. Tingle // Am Fam Physician. – 2012. – Vol. 85, No2. – P. 149-153.

128. Haerian B.S., Baum L., Kwan P., Tan, H. J., Raymond A. A., Mohamed, Z. SCN1A, SCN2A and SCN3A gene polymorphisms and responsiveness to antiepileptic drugs: a multicenter cohort study and meta-analysis // Pharmacogenomics. – 2013. – Vol. 14, № 10. – P. 1153-1166

129. Harini, C. Utility of initial EEG in first complex febrile seizure / C. Harini, E. Nagarajan, A.A. Kimia [et al.] // Epilepsy Behav. – 2015. – Vol. 52, Pt. A. – P. 200-204.

130. Hauser, W.A. The prevalence and incidence of convulsive disorders in children / W.A. Hauser // Epilepsia. – 1994. – Vol. 35, Suppl. 2. – P. S1-S6.

131. Hesdorffer, D.C. Are MRI-detected brain abnormalities associated with febrile seizure type? / D.C. Hesdorffer, S. Chan, H. Tian [et al.] // Epilepsia. – 2008. – Vol. 49, No 5. – P. 765-771.

132. Hussain, S. Febrile seizrues: demographic, clinical and etiological profile of children admitted with febrile

seizures in a tertiary care hospital / S. Hussain, S.H. Tarar // J Pak Med Assoc. – 2015. – Vol. 65, No9. – P. 1008-1010.

133. Hwang, G. Predictors of unprovoked seizure aFSer febrile seizure: short-term outcomes / G. Hwang, H.S. Kang, S.Y. Park [et al.] // Brain Dev. – 2015. – Vol. 37, No3. – P. 315-321.

134. Kaputu Kalala Malu, C. Epidemiology and characteristics of febrile seizures in children / C. Kaputu Kalala Malu, E. Mafuta Musalu, J.M. Dubru [et al.] // Rev Med Liege. - 2013. - Vol. 68, №4. - P. 180-185.

135. Kim, J. Clinical characteristics of patients with benign nonlesional temporal lobe Epilepsy / J. Kim, S.H. Kim, S.C. Lim [et al.] // Neuropsychiatr Dis Treat. – 2016. – Vol. 12. – P.1887-1891.

136. Kolfen, W. Is the long-term outcome of children following febrile convulsions favorable? / W. Kolfen, K. Pehle, S. Konig // Dev. Med. Child Neurol. – 1998.

137. Kuang Y.Q. et.al 2014

138. Laditan, A.A.O. Seizure recurrence aFSer a first febrile convulsion / A.A.O. Laditan // Ann. Trop. Paediatr. – 1994. – Vol. 14. – P. 303-308.

139. Lee, S.H. Epilepsy in children with a history of febrile seizures / S.H. Lee, J.H. Byeon, G.H. Kim [et al.] // Korean J Pediatr. – 2016. – Vol. 59, No2. – P. 74-79.

140. Lennox-Buchtal, M.A. Febrile convulsions: A reappraisal. Electroencephalogr / M.A. Lennox-Buchtal // Clin. Neuro-physiol. – 1973. – Vol. 32, Suppl. – P. 1-132.

141. Li, N. Changing trends and clinical characteristics of febrile seizures in children / N. Li, Y.Z. Chen, K.Y. Zhou // Zhongguo Dang Dai Er Ke Za Zhi. – 2015. – Vol. 17, No2. – P. 176-179.

142. Mahyar, A. Risk Factors of the First Febrile Seizures in Iranian Children / A. Mahyar, P. Ayazi, M. Fallahi [et al.] // Int J Pediatr. – 2010. – 862897. – [Epub 2010 Jun 24].

143. Millichap, J.G. Management of febrile seizures: Survey of current practice and phenobarbital usage / J.G. Millichap, J.A. Colliver // Pediatr. Neurol. – 1991. – No7. – P. 243-248.

144. Millichap, J.J. Methods of investigation and management of infections causing febrile seizures / J.J. Millichap, J. Gordon Millichap // Pediatr Neurol. – 2008. – Vol. 39, No 6. – P. 381-386.

145. Mitchell, T.V. Do Prolonged Febrile Seizures Injure the Hippocampus ? Human MRI Studies / T.V. Mitchell, D.V. Lewis // Febrile Seizures / ed.: T.Z. Baram, S. Shinnar. – San Diego [etc.] : Academic press, 2002. – P. 103-125.

146. Mulley J.C., Hodgson .B, McMahon J.M., Iona X., Bellows S., Mullen S. A., Farrell K., Mackay M., Sadleir L., Bleasel A., Gill D., Webster R., Wirrell E.C., Harbord M.,

Sisodiya S., Andermann E., Kivity S., Berkovic S.F., Scheffer I.E., Dibbens L.M. Role of the sodium channel SCN9A in genetic epilepsy with febrile seizures plus and Dravet syndrome // Epilepsia. – 2013. – Vol. 54, № 9. – P. 122-126.

147. Nilsson, G. Prevalence of Febrile Seizures, Epilepsy, and Other Paroxysmal Attacks in a Swedish Cohort of 4-Year-Old Children / G. Nilsson, E. Fernell, T. Arvidsson [et al.] // Neuropediatrics. – 2016. – Aug 14. – [Epub ahead of print].

148. Nordli Jr, D.R. Acute EEG findings in children with febrile status epilepticus: results of the FEBSTAT study / D.R. Nordli Jr, S.L. Moshé, S. Shinnar [et al.] // Neurology. – 2012. – Vol. 79, No22. – P. 2180-2186.

149. Offringa, M. Risk factors for seizure recurrence in children with febrile seizures: A pooled analysis of individual patient data from five studies / M. Offringa, P.M.M. Bossuyt, J. Lubsen [et al.] // J. Pediatr. – 1994. – Vol. 124. – P. 574-584.

150. Offringa, M. Seizures recurrence aFSer a first febrile seizures: A multivariate approach / M. Offringa, G. Derksen-Lubsen, P.M. Bossuyt [et al.] // Dev. Med. Child. Neurol. – 1992. – Vol.34. – P. 15-24.

151. Park, K.I. Role of cortical dysplasia in epileptogenesis following prolonged febrile seizure / K.I. Park, K. Chu, K.H. Jung [et al.] // Epilepsia. – 2010. – Vol. 51, No9. – P. 1809-1819.

152. Patterson J.L., Carapetian S.A., Hageman J.R., Kelley K.R. Febrile seizures // Pediatric Annals. – 2013. – Vol. 42, № 12. – P. 249-254.

153. Pavlidou, E. Febrile seizures: recent developments and unanswered questions / E. Pavlidou, C. Hagel, C. Panteliadis // Childs Nerv Syst. – 2013. – Vol. 29, No11. – P. 2011-2017.

154. Pavlidou, E. Which factors determine febrile seizure recurrence? A prospective study / E. Pavlidou, M. Tzitiridou, E. Kontopoulos [et al.] // Brain Dev. – 2008. – Vol. 30, No 1. – P. 7-13.

155. Principi, N. Vaccines and febrile seizures / N. Principi, S. Esposito // Expert Rev Vaccines. – 2013. – Vol. 12, No 8. – P. 885-892.

156. Pruna, D. Epilepsy and vaccinations: Italian guidelines / D. Pruna, P. Balestri, N. Zamponi [et al.] // Epilepsia. – 2013. – Vol. 54, Suppl 7. – P. 13-22.

157. Roulet, E. Acquired aphasia, dementia, and behavior disorder with epilepsy and continuous spike and waves during sleep in a child / E. Roulet, T. Deonna, F. Gaillard [et al.] // Epilepsia. – 1991. – Vol. 32. – P. 495-503.

158. Sadler, R.M. The syndrome of mesial temporal lobe epilepsy with hippocampal sclerosis: clinical features and differential diagnosis / R.M. Sadler // Advances in neurology.

Intractable epilepsies / eds. W.T. Blume / Philadelphia : Lippincott, 2006. – Vol. 97. – P.27-37.

159. Saghazadeh A., Mastrangelo M., Rezaei N. Genetic background of febrile seizures // Reviews in the neurosciences. – 2014. – Vol. 25, № 1. – P. 129-161.

160. Sajun Chung, M.D., Febrile seizures // Korean J Pediatr. 2014;57(9):384-395

161. Sammon, C.J. The incidence of childhood and adolescent seizures in the UK from 1999 to 2011: Aretrospective cohort study using the Clinical Practice Research Datalink / C.J. Sammon, R.A. Charlton, J. Snowball [et al.] // Vaccine. – 2015. – Vol. 33, No51. – P. 7364-7369.

162. Seinfeld, S.A. Epilepsy AFSer Febrile Seizures: Twins Suggest Genetic Influence / S.A. Seinfeld, J.M. Pellock, M.J. Kjeldsen [et al.] // Pediatr Neurol. – 2016. – Vol. 55. – P. 14-16.

163. Sfaihi, L. Febrile seizures: an epidemiological and outcome study of 482 cases / L. Sfaihi, I. Maaloul, S. Kmiha [et al.] // Childs Nerv Syst. – 2012. – Vol. 28, No10. – P. 1779-1784.

164. Shah, P.B. EEG for children with complex febrile seizures / P.B. Shah, S. James, S. Elayaraja // Cochrane Database Syst Rev. – 2015. – No12. – CD009196.

165. Sharawat, I.K. Evaluation of Risk Factors Associated with First Episode Febrile Seizure / I.K. Sharawat, J.

Singh, L. Dawman [et al.] // J Clin Diagn Res. – 2016. – Vol. 10, No5. – P. SC10-13.

166. Shi, X.L. An epidemiological survey of febrile convulsions among pupils in the Wenzhou region / X.L. Shi, Z.D. Lin, X.Y. Ye [et al.] // Zhongguo Dang Dai Er Ke Za Zhi. - 2012. - Vol. 14, № 2. - P. 128-130.

167. Shorvon, S.D. Longitudinal cohort studies of the prognosis of epilepsy: contribution of the National General Practice Study of Epilepsy and other studies / S.D. Shorvon, D.M. Goodridge // Brain. – 2013. – Vol. 136, Pt. 11. – P. 3497-3510.

168. Sofijanov, N. Febrile seizures: Clinical characteristics and ini-tial EEG / N. Sofijanov, S. Emoto, M. Kuturec [et al.] // Epilepsia. – 1992. – Vol. 33. – P. 52- 57.

169. Steinlein O.K. Mechanisms underlying epilepsies associated with sodium channel mutations //Progress in Brain Research. – 2014. – Vol. 213. – P. 97-111.

170. Talebian, A. Evaluating of knowledge, attitude, practice and related factors in mothers of children with febrile convulsion at Kashan during 2006-2007 / A. Talebian, A. Honarpisheh, B. Barekatain [et al.] // J Kashan Univ Med Sci. – 2009. – No1 (13). – P. 43-47.

171. Tarkka, R. Risk of recurrence and outcome aFSer the first febrile seizure / R. Tarkka, H. Rantala, M. Uhari [et al.] // Pediatr. Neurol. – 1998. – Vol. 18. – P. 218-220.

172. Tosun, A. Ratios of nine risk factors in children with recurrent febrile seizures / A. Tosun, G. Koturoglu, G. Serdaroglu [et al.] // Pediatr Neurol. – 2010. – Vol. 43, No 3. – P. 177-182.

173. Trinka, E. Childhood febrile convulsions—which factors determine the subsequent epilepsy syndrome? A retrospective study / E. Trinka, J. Unterrainer, U.E. Haberlandt [et al.] // Epilepsy Res. – 2002. – Vol. 50. – P. 283-292.

174. Vadlamudi L., Milne R.L., Lawrence K., Heron S.E., Eckhaus J., Keay D., Connellan M., Torn-Broers Y., Howell R.A., Mulley J.C., Scheffer I.E., Dibbens L.M., Hopper J.L., Berkovic S.F. Genetics of epilepsy: The testimony of twins in the molecular era // Neurology. – 2014. – Vol. 83, № 12. – P. 1042-1048.

175. van Stuijvenberg, M. Frequency of fever episodes related to febrile seizure recurrence / M. van Stuijvenberg, N.E. Jansen, E.W. Steyerberg [et al.] // Ada Paediatr. – 1999. – Vol. 88. – P. 52-55.

176. Van Stuljvenberg, M. Randomized, controlled trial of ibuprofen syrup administered during febrile illnesses to prevent febrile seizure recurrences / M. Van Stuljvenberg, G. Derksen-Lubsen, E.W. Steyerberg [et al.] // Pediatrics. – 1998. – Vol. 102. – P. E51.

177. Vestergaard, M. Long-term Risk of Epilepsy Following Febrile Seizures / M. Vestergaard, C.B. Pedersen,

K.M. Madsen [et al.] // Epilehsia. – 2005. – Vol. 46, Suppl. 6. – P. 81.

178. Vestergaard, M. Register-based studies on febrile seizures in Denmark / M. Vestergaard, J. Christensen // Brain Dev. – 2009. – Vol. 31, No 5. – P. 372-377.

179. Vignoli, A. Long-term outcome of epilepsy with onset in the first three years of life:Findings from a large cohort of patients / A. Vignoli, A. Peron, K. Turner [et al.] // Eur J Paediatr Neurol. – 2016. – Vol. 20, No4. – P. 566-572.

180. Visser, A.M. Febrile seizures and behavioural and cognitive outcomes in preschool children: the Generation R study / A.M. Visser, V.W. Jaddoe, A. Ghassabian [et al.] // Dev Med Child Neurol. – 2012. – Vol. 54, No 11. – P. 1006-1011.

181. Visser, A.M. Fetal growth retardation and risk of febrile seizures / A.M. Visser, V.W. Jaddoe, A. Hofman [et al.] // Pediatrics. – 2010. – Vol. 126, No 4. – P. e919-925.

182. Walsh, S. A systematic review of the risks factors associated with the onset and natural progression of epilepsy / S. Walsh, J. Donnan, Y. Fortin [et al.] // Neurotoxicology. – 2016. – Mar 19. – [Epub ahead of print]

183. Wo, S.B. Risk for developing epilepsy and epileptiform discharges on EEG in patients with febrile seizures / S.B. Wo, J.H. Lee, Y.J. Lee [et al.] // Brain Dev. – 2013. – Vol. 35, No4. – P. 307-311.

184. Yoshinaga H et al. 2013

185. Zhen-Qiang Wu, Liang Sun, Ye-Huan Sun, Cizao Ren, Yu-Hong Jiang, Xiao-Ling Lv. Interleukin 1 beta 2511 C/T gene polymorphism and susceptibility to febrile seizures: a meta-analysis // Molecular Biology Reports. 2012. Vol. 5, № 39. P. 5401—5407.

List of published scientific works.

1. Gaffarova V.F. , Khodjieva D.T. Features of the course of febrile seizures in children. // Asian Journal of Pharmaceutical and Biological Research. 2021. -P. 4-6.

2. Gaffarova V.F. Clinic-eeg correlation somatogenous of conditioned febrile seizures in children. //International Journal of Human Computing Studies.2021. –P.114-116.

3. Ходжиева Д.Т., Гаффарова В.Ф. Особенности течения фебрильных и афебрильных судорог у детей. // Журнал неврологии и нейрохирургических исследований №4.2020.-С. 57-59.

4. Khodjieva D.T., Gaffarova V.F. Clinical and neurological peculiarities of fibrileconsusions in children.// Тиббиётда янги кун. – Ташкент, 2021. - №2. -P. 266-269. .(14.00.00, №22).

5. Гаффарова В.Ф., .Ходжиева Д.Т. Особенности течения фебрильных

    судорог у детей.// Тиббиётда янги кун. – Ташкент, 2021. - №1 – С. 170-173. (14.00.00, №22).

6. Ходжиева Д.Т., Гаффарова В.Ф .Оценка фебрильных судорог в аспекте детескойневрологии.//Журнал неврологии и нейрохирургических исследований№2.2021. –С.47-49.

7. Ходжиева Д.Т., Гаффарова В.Ф .Нейропсихологическая характеристика детей с фебрильными судорогами.// Журнал

неврологии и нейрохирургических исследований.2021.-С. 260-263.

8. Маджидова Ё.Н., Гаффарова В.Ф. Прогностические критерии биллирубиновой энцефалопатии у новорожденных и младенцев.// Педиатрия научно-практический журнал №4/2021 –С. 76-78

9. Ходжиева Д.Т., Гаффарова В.Ф Характеристика фебрильных судорог у детей.// Сборник материалов и международной конференции студентов-медиков и молодых ученых. Бухара- 2021.- С-325-326.

10. Khodjieva D.T., Gaffarova V.F. The risk factors for developing febrile seizures in children.// Salon Bio& Construction Strasbourg. France 2021.-P 24-26

11. Gaffarova V.F. Characteristics of seizures children.// International journal of conference series on education and social sciences.Turkey 2021. –P. 22-23.

12. Гаффарова В.Ф, Ходжиева Д.Т. Оценка факторов риска развития фебрильных судорог у детей.// Multidiscipliner Proceedings of Digital fashion conference. Korea 2021.-P.59.

13. Гаффарова В.Ф. Способ прогнозирования психоречевых нарушений при фебрильных судорогах у детей. Методическая рекомендация. 2021.-С.18.

14. Гаффарова В.Ф. Алгоритм ведения детей с фебрильными судорогами с учетом ранней профилактики психо-речевых нарушений.Методическая рекомендация. 2021.-С.18.

15. Гаффарова В.Ф. Болаларда тутқаноқдан кейин психо-лингвистик нутқ бузилишларини аниқлаш. ЭҲМ учун дастур.DGU 20212367.

16. Gafforova V.F. Early prevention of psycho-speech disorders due to febril conversions in children// European Journal of Innovation in Nonfarmal Education/Volume2/Issuse 11/November-2022

17. Gaffarova V.F. Method for prediction of psycho-speech disorders during febril conversions in children.//ScienceAsia 48 2022. -P. 951-955 (**Scopus**)

18. Sadullayev D.I., Gaffarova V.F. Cognitive disorders in patients with acute cerebrovascular accident and arterial hypertension.// Amaliy va tibbiyot fanlar jurnali 2022.-P. 293-295.

19. Ғаффорова В.Ф. Болаларда фебрил тутқаноқнинг клиника, диагностикаси ва фебрил тутқаноқ қайталанишига олиб келувчи хавф омиллари.//Journal of Advanced Research and Stability/Volume:02 Issue:12/Dec-2022

20. Ғаффорова В.Ф. Фебрил ва афебрил хуружларнинг этиологик, клиник-неврологик ва нейрофизологик хусусиятлари.//Journal of Advanced Research and Stability/Volume:02 Issue:12/Dec-2022

1. Gafforova V.F. Aspects of febril conversions in children's neurology//European Journal of Innovation in Nonfarmal Education/Volume2/Issuse 12/December-2022

2. Gafforova V.F. Evaluate the neuropsychological, clinical-nevrological and neurophysiological characteristics of febrile and afebrile seizures//American journal of science and learning for development/Volume2/February-2023

3. Гаффарова В.Ф. Психоречевые нарушение при фебрилных судорогах у детей.// Innovation in technology and science education/Volume:2/ Issue:8/March-2023

4. Гаффарова В.Ф. Клинико-неврологические, нейрофизиологические и нейроиммунологические особенности судорожного синдрома у детей.// European Journal of Academic Research /Volume:3/ Issue:5/May-2023

LIST OF ABBREVIATIONS

AFS	afebrile seizures
ANTR	asymmetric neck tonic reflex
WHO	world health organization
IVH	intraventricular hemorrhage
ANS	autonomic nervous system
HHS	hypertension-hydrocephalus syndrome
CPCH	cerebral palsy in children
CT	computer tomography
CEEG	computer electroencephalography
LTR	labyrinthine tonic reflex
ICD-10	International classification of diseases 10
MRI	magnetic resonance imaging
SAPSA	small-amplitude polymorphic slow activity
PL	periventricular leukomalacia
COIH	consequences of intraventricular hemorrhage
SNTR	symmetrical neck tonic reflex
FS	febrile seizures
CNS	central nervous system
CN	cranial nerves
EA	epileptic activity
EEG	electroencephalography

www.ingramcontent.com/pod-product-compliance
Lightning Source LLC
LaVergne TN
LVHW010214070526
838199LV00062B/4583